THE PHONE BOOK

THE PHONE BOOK

What the telephone company would rather you not know

J. Edward Hyde

Henry Regnery Company • Chicago

Published by Henry Regnery Company
180 North Michigan Avenue, Chicago, Illinois 60601
Manufactured in the United States of America
Library of Congress Catalog Card Number: 76-6275
International Standard Book Number: 0-8092-8008-6

Published simultaneously in Canada by
Beaverbooks
953 Dillingham Road
Pickering, Ontario L1W 1Z7
Canada

CONTENTS

FOREWORD

SIXTY BILLION DOLLARS equals the combined gross national product of Belgium, Denmark, and Finland, or the cost of four years of bloodletting in the First World War, or the amount U. S. corporations paid in taxes over the past two years. In 1975, the Telephone Company had assets of just over sixty billion dollars. . . .

NINETY-THREE MILLION MILES is the distance from the earth to the sun. A ray of light traveling at 186,000 miles per second takes more than eight minutes to cover that distance. By 1974, the Telephone Company was using enough cable and wire to reach from the earth to the sun—and back again—three times, with several million miles to spare. . . .

TWENTY-FIVE STATES lie between the Atlantic Ocean and the Mississippi River. The Telephone Company has used enough plastic in the manufacture of telephone sets to cover all twenty-five with one quarter inch of high-impact unbreakable styrene. . . .

IN FIVE YEARS, 157,680,000 seconds of time pass into history. In 1973, the Telephone Company handled one long distance call for every second of time in a five-year period. . . .

IN 1973, Chrysler, A & P, R C A, Phillips Petroleum, S. S. Kresge, Boeing, International Harvester, Woolworth's, Greyhound, Firestone, Litton, and General Foods, among others, each reported annual profits of less than $150,000,000. In that same year, the Telephone Company wrote off—as being uncollectable—debts of $150,000,000. . . .

Section I: THE COMPANY

"*If Bell had known anything about electricity, he never would have invented the telephone. . . .*"—*Moses Farmer, scientist.*

The world's largest corporation can credit its founding and subsequent success to suspect patents, Mr. Bell's ignorance of electricity and the German language, and what can only be described as incredible good fortune. On reviewing the facts, it becomes readily apparent that Somebody Up There obviously liked Bell and his organization, although no one is quite sure why. . . .

1

The Bell System

In 1837, an American named C. G. Page discovered the principle of electronic sound transmission that is the key to the operation of the telephone. By magnetizing and demagnetizing a lightning rod, Page managed to coax unintelligible sounds from the rod. Although he had no way of knowing just how valuable his contribution was to the unborn industry, his discovery formed the basis for its future development. Page himself made no further contribution to the telephone. In fact, it would be 1861 before any additional progress was made.

In that year, Professor Philipp Reis of the University of Frankfurt became the first man actually to transmit distinct sound. He invented the electrically activated diaphragm. The means used to achieve this were somewhat unorthodox even by the scientific standards of the day. Reis wrapped a sausage skin around a beer cork. After wrapping wire around a knitting needle and laying it across the top of a violin, he then connected the two parts with wire and put an acid-cell bat-

3

tery in the middle. With the power turned on, Reis's contraption worked just as he thought it would; when the beer cork was thumped, the knitting needle's jolting reaction caused the violin strings to vibrate. But what the professor hadn't suspected was that when the process was reversed—when the needle was drawn across the violin—sounds would emanate from the beer cork. From a purely technical standpoint, the telephone was born at the instant Reis first threw the switch, for his apparatus was able to receive and transmit sound—which is all a telephone is able to do. The only thing missing from Reis's machine was the ability to transmit voices. Had Reis taken the time to develop his idea further, there is every reason to believe the telephone might be fifteen years older and its inventor German. He came as close as anyone could to inventing the telephone without actually doing so. As it was, Alexander Bell, who would receive credit for the telephone's invention, was not even aware of Reis's work until after he invented the telephone. Part of Mr. Bell's ignorance might be attributed to a bad experience with yet another German scientist's work. But then, he had no beer corks and sausage to experiment with, either.

The German scientist in question, Hermann von Helmholtz, probably never knew that he caused Alexander Bell to charge off on a wild-goose chase. He might not have cared if he had. Yet, indirectly, he must receive some credit for the telephone's development. For without his influence Bell's interest in the electronic transmission of sound might never have developed.

Von Helmholtz directed his energies toward the creation of intelligent sound through the use of electrically charged tuning forks. Although he never actually accomplished this goal, he wrote a paper on the subject that was published in a widely read scientific journal. In Scotland, seventeen-year-old Alexander Bell read a copy of this report and, somewhat misguidedly, began the experiments that would lead to his invention of the telephone.

The journal, published in German, clearly described what von Helmholtz had been trying to do, but unfortunately Alexander Bell's grasp of German was not on a par with his knowledge of electronics. He understood the treatise to mean that von Helmholtz had been trying to send words by telegraph by using the aforementioned tuning forks. After Bell had spent nearly a year trying to recreate the impossible, an acquaintance whose German was more formidable than his corrected his assumption and Bell abandoned his efforts. The only positive result of his misguided experimentations was the assurance that Bell's interest in electronic transmissions would not diminish.

His efforts with tuning forks had been aimed at improving telegraphy. After migrating to Boston, his tactics changed but not the goal. He was still not thinking in terms of voice transmission.

To earn a living in this country, Alexander Bell became a teacher of the deaf. In fact, his initial fame as a highly effective teacher arrived long before he became a successful—if accident-prone—inventor. He was one of the first teachers to use the one-on-one teacher-pupil concept, and although he continued his experiments in his leisure hours there can be no doubt that he always considered teaching to be his main contribution to society. Very late in life, when the telephone was an established fact throughout the world, a newspaper reporter asked him what he considered to be his greatest achievement in life. Bell replied simply, "I was a teacher of the deaf." It was while he was teaching deaf students that he met the men with whom he would form American Telephone and Telegraph: Gardiner Hubbard and Thomas Sanders.

Their children were students of Alexander Bell. Through his close working relationship with the families of his students, these two men became aware of his electrical experiments and, impressed with his abilities as a teacher, they listened raptly to his descriptions of the possibilities of sound transmission. In 1871 Bell persuaded them to form a partnership, with Hubbard and Sanders supplying the money and Bell supplying the work. Profits would be split three ways. Thus the conception of what we know today as A. T. & T. was formalized with a mere handshake. With the backing of these two men, Bell was able to spend more time and money on his experiments. In fact, he was able to hire a helper whose name was Thomas Watson.

Initially, Bell and Watson did not even consider the possibility of inventing a telephone. Although they discussed "sending voices electrographically," all of their early efforts were directed toward the perfection of a "harmonic telegraph," a device that they hoped would revolutionize telegraphy. It undoubtedly would have, had they succeeded. At the time telegraphs could not send while receiving, and vice versa. Nor could more than one dot or dash be sent at the same time. The goal of Bell and Watson was somehow to find a way for more than one signal to be sent at once and for simultaneous sending and receiving. They believed it could be done. So did Hubbard and Sanders, but only because Bell told them it was possible. Hubbard and Sanders were businessmen, not scientists, and it is highly doubtful whether they would have subsidized Bell in a search for something so elusive as "electrographic voice transmission." If Bell had any serious misgivings on the matter, he wisely kept them to himself.

Still, things change. Although they had been enthusiastic about Bell's harmonic telegraph in 1871, the next four and a half years dampened Hubbard and Sanders' spirits considerably. Their investment in Bell's experiments was money they felt they were not likely to see again, for the inventor had nothing to show for his pains except a clutter of useless equipment in his workshop. In Bell's working journals of 1875, in fact, we find indications that had matters remained stagnant both investors might have pulled out in 1876. Overenthusiasm on Watson's part prevented this from happening.

On June 2, 1875, Watson tightened a screw one full turn instead of only one half turn and, in doing so, screwed down a sounding reed so that it touched the pole of an electromagnet. By chance, Bell happened to be working in another room near the receiver. When Watson's reed touched the magnet, it squawked, Bell heard it, and the first practical diaphragm was invented. Both men immediately recognized the importance of this find, which Professor Reis in Frankfurt accomplished fourteen years earlier. All work on the harmonic telegraph stopped (although this is what they continued to call the device), and their full attention was directed toward the development of "electrographic" sound transmission.

It took eight more months of experimentation before Bell had his telephone. On February 14, 1876, he filed for a patent on his device, and within the month patent number 174,456 was granted to Alexander Bell. Three days later, in the famous "Watson, come here. I want you" scene, he actually made his telephone work. However, one wonders what actually transpired. The known facts are that Watson did hear Bell summon him from another room via the telephone when Bell spilled acid on his trousers. And although Bell has been credited with uttering two of the most laconic declarative sentences in the history of American technology, our knowledge of human nature tells us that one does not calmly request the presence of an associate when battery acid is burning through the crotch of one's drawers. The exact words of what must have been a frantic statement of fact are lost forever. "Watson, come here. I want you" sounds like the work of an early-day public relations man.

Most of the legal problems that were to entangle Bell and his company over the next seventeen years would be due to the fact that he got his patent before he had a working device. The first of these court battles involved Alexander Bell and a man named Elisha Gray.

Gray had been working on the harmonic telegraph at the same time that Bell had. He had even filed a caveat on his device in January of 1876, notifying the government of his intention to patent his invention, but his application was denied because Bell's patent had been accepted first. Gray had been heartbreakingly close. Bell received his patent only hours before Gray walked into the same patent office to find that his caveat had been denied. When he became aware of the facts surrounding the patenting of Bell's device, he understandably sought rectification in the courts.

Gray pointed out that what Bell had was not a harmonic

telegraph, even though this is what Bell called his device. He also drew attention to the fact that Bell had yet to coax a syllable out of his machine when he received his patent. But because he felt that his case was already strong enough, he neglected to mention that Bell had in effect perjured himself when filing the affidavit accompanying his patent application. In light of subsequent events, Gray might well have done so.

While Gray complained to the courts, Bell and his associates were busy making money from the controversial patent tucked away in their safe. They were also reorganizing their company. First of all, a new split was agreed to. Bell, Hubbard, and Sanders would each receive 30% of the profits. Thomas Watson, for his loyal service, would receive 10%.

It was also decided at that time that Bell and Watson would take their harmonic telegraph on tour to raise money. This first tour, covering the northeastern part of the United States, was highly successful. After demonstrating their crackerbox-like telephone to audiences in theaters throughout that section of the country, 700 orders were received.

In March of 1877, Gray's protests grew louder. Bell and his associates, in an effort to silence Gray, made him an offer that apparently was one he couldn't refuse. They offered Gray the opportunity to take his harmonic telegraph with them on their next telephone demonstration tour. Gray, a perennial also-ran in telephone history, agreed to their terms. In April of 1877, Alexander Bell and Elisha Gray went on tour, with Bell selling his telephone and Gray's telegraph. Gray's only task during this odyssey was to admit as often as possible that Alexander Bell had invented the telephone.

In the meantime, momentous events were taking place back in Massachusetts. Hubbard and Sanders devised the formula that would lead to the Bell Company's becoming the giant corporation it is today. In May the Bell Company partners announced that henceforth their equipment could be leased, not bought. Terms were available for anyone who cared to lease a phone.

No one can shortcredit this visionary policy established at

a time when there were no more than three thousand phones in existence, for without the lease clause the Bell Company would not have achieved the size that it has. Hubbard and Sanders were unencumbered by Bell's sense of social conscience. They did not see the telephone as a scientific contribution for the betterment of mankind. They were, one might say, only in it for the money, and the lease clause guaranteed that there would always be a continuing supply of it coming into the company's strongboxes. Had anyone been able to tell these two businessmen that, one hundred years hence, every American would have access to a telephone, they would probably have been singularly unimpressed. But if they had been told that their lease clause arrangement would eventually generate twenty billion dollars a year in accounts receivable, it might have been hard to restrain their joy.

Even after the announcement of the leasing policy, Hubbard and Sanders weren't really sold on the idea of owning a telephone company. In July of 1877, the first Bell Telephone Company was organized. In September, Hubbard offered to sell it to Western Union for $100,000 in the hope of making a not unreasonable return on his investment before the madness ran its course. Western Union had an even lower opinion of the telephone than Hubbard did. It declined the offer.

But by March of 1878, Western Union had good cause to change its mind. For in that month, a wholly owned subsidiary of Western Union, the Gold and Stock Telegraph Company, took out its telegraph equipment and began using the Bell Company's telephones. After being snubbed when it offered ten times the previous amount for the Bell Company, Western Union decided to drive Bell out of business. The wild free-for-all that followed was the first of two major Telephone Wars.

Bell and his associates, aware of what Western Union was planning, made frantic efforts to prepare for the onslaught. First, they hired a professional manager, Theodore Vail, to run the company. Vail was a former executive of the postal service, and he brought to the fledgling business the acumen and common sense the company badly needed. Second, the

Bell Company reorganized once more in order to raise money
to cover the cost of the war. From that point, all it could do
was sit back. The next move would be Western Union's, and
Bell did not have long to wait.

Within a month, Western Union bought the rights to the
telephone apparatus manufactured by Elisha Gray and A. E.
Dolbear. Gray, having reconsidered his position after his
tour with Alexander Bell, reneged on the deal he had made
with the Bell Company. Dolbear brought to the union an in-
duction coil much superior to that used in the Bell Company
phones. As if this weren't enough, Western Union hired Thomas Edison to further improve its product. He promptly did
so by inventing a carbon transmitter that enabled the phone
user to talk in a normal tone of voice. This was no small improvement; at the time it was necessary to yell at the top of
your lungs if you wished to be heard on a Bell telephone.
These early phones did not work like the ones we have today.
In fact, they worked much like the tin-can-on-a-string toys
that most children play with. The telephone was not very
complex. It connected you with only one other telephone and
it did not have a bell. In fact, if you wished to ring up the party
on the other end you were provided with a thumper. The
thumper made a noise you hoped would be heard by the party
who had the telephone on the other end of your line. With
room for improvement everywhere, Edison's transmitter was
a technical triumph.

The Bell Company's feeble countermeasures took the form
of a highly questionable act. Within a month after Edison's
carbon transmitter went into production for Western Union,
the Bell Company announced that it, too, had a carbon transmitter. Francis Blake is credited with inventing this device,
although it was so similar to the one Edison invented that at
first Bell was refused a patent on it. It did work better than
the one invented by Edison, however. The voice transmission
was much clearer and far more distinct than his. Western Union accused Bell of stealing, but no one believed that Bell
could do such a thing. The fact that the initial patent application on the Bell transmitter was denied does not prove that

the Bell Company plagiarized Edison's blueprints. It only means that someone in the patent office thought Edison's and Blake's devices were substantially similar.

When Bell achieved technical parity, Western Union tried a different approach. It barred the Bell Company from using its line right-of-ways and, at the same time, organized its own telephone company, The American Speaking Telephone Company.

The Bell Company countered this move in two ways. First, it filed suit against Western Union for patent infringement. Second, it began thinking strongly of starting its own telegraph company. Jay Gould, noted financier and scoundrel, offered to help Bell accomplish this goal, but the Telephone War ended before such a company could be organized.

After studying the situation through the spring of 1879, the Supreme Court of the United States reached a compromise decision that neither side liked but both promised to adhere to. First, the court determined that Bell, not Gray, invented the telephone. Second, Western Union was directed to sell its 56,000 telephones in fifty-five cities in return for 20 percent of the Bell Company's profits over the next seventeen years. The Bell Company was ordered to stay out of the telegraph business and not to compete in any area then being served by Western Union. Upon this basis, the Telephone War was ended. With no major potential threat remaining, the path was now clear for the growth of the giant we know today as the American Telephone and Telegraph Company.

Mad days of trial and error

A reorganization of the Bell Company in 1879 changed the name to the National Bell Telephone Company. One year later, the need for additional capital brought on yet another reorganization, and this time the name was changed to the American Bell Telephone Company. The Bell Company was not merely concerned with raising the additional capital, however. Both reorganizations served to nullify franchise agreements contracted before the Bell Company knew what a lucrative proposition it had going for it. Bell offered to renegotiate all of these agreements, but the terms were so weighted in the company's favor that the offers sounded more like a demand for unconditional surrender. Bell offered five-year contracts, breakable at Bell's option, with the following stipulations: Bell could buy back any equipment at cost or less; Bell had an option on stock control; Bell assumed ownership of all inventions and other developments made by the franchisee; and the franchisee could have nothing to do with independent suppliers. This last clause was inserted because Bell wished to protect its investment in Western Electric.

Western Electric was formed in 1869 by Enos Barton and none other than that noted telephone pioneer, Elisha Gray. Western Union bought control of the company during the Telephone War, and Bell bought control from Western Union in 1879 after the telephone/telegraph compromise in the courts. The working arrangement Bell made with Western Electric is still the guiding philosophy today. Bell agreed to buy all equipment made by Western Electric, which agreed to sell all its equipment to Bell at cost. This exercise in corporate incest has resulted in no less than four attempts by the federal government to delve into the deep recesses of the Bell Company's monopolistic practices. All four have failed. So far.

The first study, undertaken in 1934, did not succeed in separating Bell and Western, but it did result in the formation of the F. C. C. (the Federal Communications Commission), the government watchdog supposed to regulate and supervise the activities of all corporations and organizations engaged in communications activities in the United States. The second study, undertaken in 1949, plodded along for two and a half years before being abandoned by a Dixiecrat/Republican-dominated congress. Officially, no evidence of wrongdoing could be found. However, a congressional subcommittee stated that the government's action in settling the case was a "blot on the enforcement history of the antitrust laws" and that it was based in part on "misrepresentations" by the F. C. C. A third study, undertaken in 1956 by a Democratic congress short on party funds, resulted in an unbelievable whitewash. Congress ruled that the Bell patents must be licensed at reasonable prices—but that Bell could decide who could receive such largess. Congress didn't stop there. Not only could Congress find nothing wrong with the Bell-Western arrangement, it actually gave its blessing to the very practices it had initially meant to stop. In late 1956, it was ruled that non-Bell suppliers had no right to buy from Western Electric unless the Bell System chose to let them buy.

This last clause must have astounded non-Bell companies as much as it pleased the Bell System. For nineteen years more, price gouging continued with the blessings of the government. Then, in December of 1974, the Justice Department filed suit to forcibly sever Western Electric from the Bell System. In spite of the fact that no decision is expected until sometime in the 1980s, we cannot expect that this fourth attack will turn out differently from previous attempts. This time, economic rather than political factors may come into play.

On the day the Justice Department announced its intention of filing suit, a weak stock market attempting a rally suddenly dropped 2½ points. Market analysts, already harried by economic considerations not attributable to the Bell suit, understandably prefer not to think of the consequences if the government actually forced Ma Bell and her daughter to part company. In all probability, the Bell System stock, the most widely held stock on the market today, would plummet, dragging other stocks down with it. In times of economic uncertainty, we can no more afford a stock market crash than we can a nuclear war.

From franchise to operating company in 20 short years

Theodore Vail's tightfisted offers of franchises had more takers than franchises, which caused the Bell Company to wonder whether it had once again been too largehearted. Rather than call the franchises in—which might have shaken confidence in the organization—the Bell Company decided to buy them up. But Bell was unable to do this immediately; there were several stumbling blocks in the way. One of the biggest was the uncertain future of the company itself.

Ever since 1879, the Bell Company had been in court. In fact, Bell would be involved in nearly 600 lawsuits during its first seventeen years of existence. The company won every one of these lawsuits, but a few decisions were uncomfortably close. The closest Bell ever came to losing in court was a suit filed by one Daniel Drawbaugh of Pennsylvania in 1888. Mr. Drawbaugh's suit contended that he had invented the telephone in 1867. He had a score of credible witnesses on his side of the case and actually won the lower court decisions. Naturally, Bell appealed these decisions. But only by a narrow 4-to-3 decision in the Supreme Court of the United States did it prevail. The minority report of Justice Bradley is historically interesting because it shows that not everyone was ready to accept the Gospel of the Bell Company:

> We think that Daniel Drawbaugh anticipated the invention of Mr. Bell. . . . It is perfectly natural for the world to take the part of the man who has already achieved national eminence. So it was with Bell and Drawbaugh. . . . We think Bell's patent is void by the anticipations of Drawbaugh.

This close call, following Drawbaugh's victory in the lower courts, gave credence to the rumors that Bell had bribed someone on the High Court bench. But of course they were only rumors.

The next barrier in Bell's path of total domination of the telephone market would have stopped a lesser organization completely: The initial patent was due to expire in 1894. But by that time, several thousand Bell patents prevented others from getting into the market with anything other than the original boxlike telephone device. The Bell Company's policy of patenting everything it invented, designed, improved, and established prevented the wholesale slaughter that had been predicted by major investors. But it did nothing to encourage the franchisees to sell out. Clearly a different approach was needed.

In 1897 another reorganization established the American

Telephone and Telegraph Company that we have today. Two years later rumors that the company was on the verge of bankruptcy panicked many investors, particularly those of subsidiaries. It appeared that the company was overextended financially and unable to meet service obligations and that—after having brushed aside major blows from the outside—the Bell organization was about to collapse from within. Supposedly more out of charity than anything else, A. T. & T. offered to buy up shares of the subsidiaries. Many franchisees gratefully sold out to the parent firm. Over the passage of the years we can see what put the smile on the face of the A. T. & T. tiger. The smooth maneuverings of A. T. & T.'s top executives cannot be given enough credit. They accomplished the complete takeover and control of the franchisees, a move begun eighteen years before, without creating so much as a corporate ripple. When what had happened became clear, the former holders of franchises howled, but there was nothing to be done. Once again, the Bell Company had emerged slightly bruised but the winner, having repelled the attacks of its competitors and double-crossed its own people. Now the organization turned to other targets. For example, there was an old score to settle with the Western Union Company.

After reaching the compromise agreement with Western Union in 1879, Bell had other real and imagined enemies to worry about and so did not at first concern itself with its former arch rival. Western Union, too, believing that Bell was honorably living up to its end of the agreement, went its own way. Then one day in 1910 Western Union discovered that the Bell organization was its major stockholder; under the cover of its subsidiaries, A. T. & T. had quietly bought up every share of Western Union stock that had appeared in the late fall of 1909. For the ensuing six years, Bell enthusiastically milked both the public and Western Union itself. But this was the era of trustbusting and in 1917, at the pointed urging of the government, the Bell System agreed to sell its interest in Western Union and to forever afterward leave it alone. Bell also was urged to quit buying up stock belonging to its competitors in the phone market, and, realizing that territories worth invading were becoming fewer every year, Bell agreed. But by then Bell had turned a critical organizational eye toward its own family and decided that it needed an overhaul.

In 1911, A. T. & T. organized its subsidiaries into the operating companies we have today. The chart printed here lists these companies and shows how much interest A. T. & T. owns in each of them. What this chart does not show are companies and corporations in which the Bell System's interest is small, foreign investments, and subsidiaries of subsidiaries. Such a listing would be nine times as long, for the Bell System has direct interests in at least 276 organizations, many of them not related to the telephone industry. Control of these organizations is maintained in a pyramid fashion. Bell also has interlocking financial arrangements with such corporations as the Chase Manhattan Bank, IBM, Prudential Insurance, Sears Roebuck, General Motors, the U. S. Steel Company, and Lever Brothers. Should the need arise, the Bell System could exercise control of *400 billion dollars,* fully one third of this country's entire 1974 gross national product.

The Organization

In the words of Theodore Vail, Bell's aim is "One System, One Policy, Universal Service." On the level of actual practice, this may be paraphrased to include "Maximum Control for Maximum Profit." How Bell controls its operating divisions makes J. D. Rockefeller's efforts at controlling the oil industry look like the feeble efforts of a novice Monopoly player. Simply put, the Bell System receives profits as the manufacturer through Western Electric, and profits on the consumer level as the operating company.

The Bell empire has four basic components: American Telephone and Telegraph, the operating companies listed on the following page (there are twenty-two of these in which Bell owns a minimum of 86% of the stock), Western Electric, and the Bell Laboratories. There is actually a fifth cog in this

American Telephone and Telegraph

Subsidiary	Capital Stock owned by A. T. & T.
New England Tel. & Tel. Co.	71.4%
New York Tel. Co.	100.0%
New Jersey Bell Tel. Co.	100.0%
Bell Tel. Co. of Pennsylvania	100.0%
Diamond State Tel. Co.	100.0%
Chesapeake & Potomac Tel. Co.	100.0%
Chesapeake & Potomac Tel. Co. of Maryland	100.0%
Chesapeake & Potomac Tel. Co. of Virginia	100.0%
Chesapeake & Potomac Tel. Co. of W. Virginia	100.0%
Southern Bell Tel. and Tel. Co.	100.0%
South Central Bell Tel. Co.	100.0%
Ohio Bell Tel. Co.	100.0%
Michigan Bell Tel. Co.	100.0%
Indiana Bell Tel. Co., Inc.	100.0%
Wisconsin Tel. Co.	100.0%
Northwestern Bell Tel. Co.	100.0%
Southwestern Bell Tel. Co.	100.0%
Illinois Bell Tel. Co.	100.0%
Mountain States Tel. & Tel. Co.	86.8%
Pacific Northwest Bell Tel. Co.	89.2%
Pacific Tel. & Tel. Co.	90.2%
Bell Tel. Co. of Nevada[1]	-----
Western Electric Co., Inc.	100.0%
195 Broadway Corporation	100.0%
Bell Telephone Laboratories, Inc.[2]	50.0%
Southern New England Tel. Co.	17.7%
Cincinnati & Suburban Bell Tel. Co.	26.5%
Bell Tel. Co. of Canada	2.2%
ComSat Corp.	29.0%
Nassau Smelting & Refining Co., Inc.	100.0%
Teletype Corp.	100.0%
Sandia Corp.	100.0%
Manufacturer's Junction Ry. Co.	100.0%
Bellcomm, Inc.[2]	50.0%

1. Wholly owned subsidiary of Pacific Tel. & Tel. Co.
2. The other 50.0% is owned by Western Electric.

wheel, A. T. & T. Long Lines, but this is an extension of the American Telephone and Telegraph Company and will be covered as such later.

The American Telephone and Telegraph Company is the largest holding company ever organized. Compared to the Bell System, giant Gulf and Western is a mere stone on a mountainside. The American Telephone and Telegraph Company holds all of the stock owned by the Bell System, sets all policies for the Bell System, decides what financial policies will be followed by the Bell System, and collects and distributes all information for the Bell System. Should the management of any one of its divisions act independently, A. T. & T. assumes the mantle of a feudal lord rendering a decision. Its power is absolute. If by some wild happenstance an operating company were to revolt and make a decision on its own, A. T. & T. could effectively isolate the rebel by closing off its financial pipeline and shutting down its outgoing circuits, courtesy of Long Lines. (Long Lines is responsible for the long distance telephone circuits under the ground, on the poles, and through inner space via the microwave system. Although all long distance circuits fall under its jurisdiction, Long Lines takes no independent action. It belongs to A. T. & T.)

All personnel in the Bell System are under A. T. & T.'s tight control. The machinations of the parent firm determine what manager will work where. Although most management people will spend their working days in the division where they started, those tapped for leadership may work for as many as twenty different Bell companies before reaching the pinnacle of success. Bell denies the existence of the so-called "manager list," but every Bell manager hopes his name is on it. It, too, is the property of A. T. & T. Nor does A. T. & T. allow any latitude for independent action on the part of its employees. Each of the one million-plus employees is known, numbered, and watched. The Bell System is not just a name. It is a two-word description of a process that takes individuals and turns them into so many interchangeable parts.

A Bell operator in Texas receives the same training as an operator in California. A Bell employee can leave his job in New York on Friday and pick up where he left off on Monday morning in a San Francisco office. The Bell System has, for over two years, offered its employees the opportunity to move around the country under the auspices of the "It's-your-move" plan. Such a program would not be possible without the thorough standardization practiced by the Bell System. Standardization applies to the purchase of pencils, so it should not be surprising to learn that everything else Bell people do and use is standardized as well. A. T. & T. publishes a guidebook and updates it annually. In this bible, known as the "Joint Practices," every conceivable task is categorized, indexed, and worded so that the most obtuse employee can follow it. This book is distributed to Bell offices everywhere by A. T. & T. For this service and others, A. T. & T. receives from its operating companies royalties in the amount of 1% a year of gross profits.

The operating companies, twenty-two in all, are the local representatives of A. T. & T. They provide local service to subscribers and conduct all Bell System business on a regional level. The operating companies range in size from the minuscule Cincinnati & Suburban Bell Telephone Company to the mammoth Southwestern Bell Telephone Company, largest in the chain. In terms of personnel, the operating companies are the farm clubs where new talent is discovered and developed for future positions of responsibility throughout the system. These companies formulate no policies, institute no services, and take no position harmful to the whole. They are nothing more than regional divisions of the A. T. & T. organization.

If this is so, then why isn't there just one big corporation with regional divisions? Well, this is for all intents and purposes exactly what A. T. & T. is. The reasons such an arrangement has never been formally recognized have to do with state laws and human psychology.

The laws of many states prohibit out-of-state corporations from owning and operating state utilities. Technically, there is no direct relationship between A. T. & T. and its subsidiaries, at least not one that existing state laws can do anything about.

The second reason American Telephone and Telegraph

never formally adopted its children is that such a national
organization would be far too big, not from a management
standpoint but from the standpoint of the customer's psyche.
The idea of a national utility with 60 billion dollars in its
coffers could not be emotionally tolerated by most people. It
would be too large, too powerful, too suspect. But most people will tolerate something the size of Pacific Telephone and
Telegraph, or the Cincinnati and Suburban Bell Telephone
Company, because they're small enough to comprehend. The
operating companies give the Bell System the appearance of
being home-grown. If you doubt the importance of this, ask
twenty strangers what they think of the idea of having a national telephone company. This is exactly what we have now,
but it is very effectively camouflaged by the operating companies.

The only subsidiary nationwide in scope is Western Electric. Western Electric manufactures all of the Bell System's
equipment and sells it to the Bell System at cost. If inflation
begins to gnaw at Western Electric's profit margin, American
Telephone and Telegraph simply raises the cost. Western
Electric has no say in the matter. The operating companies
can then point to the increased cost of Western Electric's
equipment when asking for a rate increase for themselves.
This arrangement has worked nicely for 96 years.

Western Electric is the largest of all the Bell subsidiaries,
employing thirty percent of the Bell System's total work
force. It has twenty-five plants strategically located throughout the United States and Canada. Some of these locations
reputedly conceal stockpiles of civil defense equipment not
necessarily limited to the crackers and bottled water that can
be found in most fallout shelters. In the event of a nuclear
attack, twenty-five warheads may very well be addressed to
the Western Electric Company, which ought to interest those
persons living nearby.

The last of American Telephone and Telegraph's basic
units is Bell Laboratories. The largest pure research center in
the world, Bell Labs can claim credit for the invention of the

transistor, the digital computer, and most telephone hardware back to, but not including, the hand crank. The people at Bell Labs are productive. Nearly a thousand patents each year are issued in the Bell System's name. This not only creates an image of intensive creativity, it effectively prohibits potential competitors and customers from operating without dispensation from the Bell System.

The four parts of the Bell System have one important factor in common other than their bloodline. Each places great emphasis on local-level activities. Whether it be in New York City or Mena, Arkansas, the Bell System does its best to ingratiate itself locally. Unlike other large interest groups, the Bell System does not seek the favors of those at the top. The Bell System does just the opposite and its effectiveness speaks for itself. The Bell System's win-lose ratio is better than that of UCLA's basketball team. By retaining many local law firms, Bell keeps local politicians in line. By flooding local civic groups with its employees, Bell manages to keep local public relations always in a favorable light. For example, you know Bill Jones who works for the Bell System; he is a great bowler and human being. So is Mary, and Jack, and ninety-eight percent of the remaining 999,998 employees. You see these nice people and assume the company is as nice as they are. Unfortunately for all of us, there is very little relationship between the policies of the organization and the personalities of the people who work for it.

The Independents

If the telephone industry is represented by the face of a clock, 9 hours and 50 minutes constitute the Bell System's share. The remaining 2 hours and 10 minutes belong to the other 1,832 telephone companies.

Background

The Phone War of 1878 resulted in the formation of two nationwide communications monopolies: Western Union's telegraph and the Bell Company's telephone. Although Western Union's monopoly survived almost unchallenged until Bell's attempted takeover in 1910, Bell's telephone monopoly lasted less than a year. Most competitors disappeared as soon as the Bell Company filed suit against them for patent infringement, but at least 1,730 telephone companies were organized and operated during the period when Bell was supposed to have an exclusive mandate. When the original patent expired in 1894, this number quadrupled. In its charming history of the telephone industry as it sees it, the Bell System states that:

> Independent companies sprang up everywhere, often in towns where Bell companies operated. Speculators started companies on shoestrings, selling stocks of dubious worth and offering impossibly low rates in order to steal Bell Customers.[1]

While it is true that some of these independents were started "on shoestrings" and offered low rates, let it not be forgotten whose shady dealings with the unscrupulous Jay Gould had to be stopped by the Supreme Court. From all available evidence, the birth of the independent telephone industry was due more to the Bell Company's mismanagement than to the greed of shady speculators.

Even in the early days, Bell & Co. envisioned a nationwide telephone system. In 1878, the farsighted Alexander Bell wrote:

> ... I believe that in the future, wires will unite the head offices of the Telephone Company in different cities, and that a man in one part of the country may communicate by word of mouth with another in a distant place.

Bell's use of the words "Telephone Company" leaves little doubt that he saw his small company as becoming the sole provider of telephone service in the nation, if not the world. With patent in hand and its almost incredible record in the

---

1. An Introduction to the Bell System, Chapter 3, page 1.

courts (600 wins-0 losses), the Bell Company set out to fulfill Alexander's prophecy. But it did so with a soon-to-be-characteristic disregard for customer demand, and this proved to be its undoing.

Because the Bell Company had no legally recognized competition, it could go where profits were greatest to set up companies. For its services it could charge any rate the market would bear. Marginally profitable areas could be ignored until the company was ready to enter them. The singular worship of profits so disgusted Theodore Vail that he left the Bell Company in 1887. As a parting shot, he wrote:

> We have a duty to the public at large to make our service as good as possible and as universal as possible, and that earnings should be used not only to reward investors for their investment but also to accomplish these objectives.

Bell management thanked him for his comments and wished him a happy retirement. Those he left behind had neither his visionary business sense nor his sensible principles of customer service. Ignoring the protests of customers regarding exorbitant rates and the pleas of rural areas for service at any price, Bell's leadership plundered selected profitable areas during the remaining years of their exclusive ownership without realizing that they were pinning a target on their own chest in the neglected regions. Undoubtedly Bell's management suspected that bad times lay just on the other side of the initial patent expiration. Incredibly, they did nothing to prevent the deluge.

In the cities where the Bell had its biggest stake, competitors appeared on nearly every corner. In 1894 and 1895, some 6,000 telephone companies were established in cities where Bell was already providing service. Nearly all hoped to capitalize on the Bell Company's high cost of service. Most of these rebel companies had brief lifespans simply because capital requirements were larger than their capabilities, and they were rapidly consumed. Those independents able to accumulate capital reserves and operate on a regular basis were also consumed, only it took a little longer.

The Bell Company would first offer to buy these small but solvent enterprises. Not surprisingly, quite often the offer would be refused. If this happened, Bell unmasked its big guns. The most widely used tactic was to start a price war the little company could not hope to win. The reason it could not win was because the Bell Company's idea of a price cut was to offer free service for as long as it proved necessary. Since these small companies had no way of matching Bell's nationwide financial base, they vanished like a lamb in a ravenous wolfpack.

In those rare instances where the small company could join the free-service-for-all-comers game, the Bell Company resorted to other measures: refusing to share line right-of-ways, publicly denouncing the competitor's service and equipment, and, if all else failed, sabotage. Although both sides were guilty of destroying equipment belonging to the other, we can't hear both sides of the story today because the only surviving party flatly denies that any such activities took place. Just about the only souvenir we have of such battles is a short paragraph in the Bell System Code of Conduct pertaining to the responsibility of every employee to protect company property and equipment. Although it is supposed to apply only in times of war, it was first printed in an era when Bell was at war with its competitors, when mysterious fires and broken lines were daily occurrences in the battle zones.

The Bell System fought well if not cleanly in the urban sectors and retained control wherever it had already been prior to the patent expiration. In rural areas where Bell arrived after the competition was well established, the victory column was markedly shorter.

The Bell Company had nonchalantly ignored the rural areas with good reason—there was not enough money to be made there. Consequently, rural telephone companies had an easier time than did their city-based brethren. It didn't take much to get started, either. In some instances, two orders and $100 were all that was needed for the village blacksmith and the horse doctor to become founders of the first local telephone exchange. By 1897 more than 1,000 rural telephone exchanges had been organized to fill the void left by the negligent Bell, then heavily engaged in the aforementioned urban price war. Once the Bell Company overcame its city-based resistance, it directed its energies to the destruction of the weaker farm systems. Apparently it never occurred to Bell that there might be a difference between competitors motivated primarily by profit and competitors concerned solely with providing service. Or that tactics designed to eliminate one might cause the other to flourish.

In farm areas, the Bell found that price slashing didn't work. Farm telephone systems had two inherent qualities that worked against Bell no matter what Bell did. First of all, rural exchange pricing was more than reasonable before the Bell Company got into town. Having little else to go on, most rural telephone systems were organized on a cooperative basis guaranteeing low consumer prices. The second advantage was a by-product of the first: loyalty. No matter how low Bell prices were, loyalty and kinship to the local telephone masters overcame the lure of cheaper service. Nor did sabotage work as it had in the cities. In communities where everyone knew everyone else, the Bell System's bullyboys were notably conspicuous. In one community where Bell's terror tactics were employed, a retaliatory fire in the local Bell office raged out of control while the Bell representative wrung his hands. In response to his call for help, one thoughtful soul handed him a water pail and told him where the community well was located. Meanwhile, the Bell System goons languished in the local jail on charges of vagrancy and missed all the excitement.

In a final effort to eliminate these durable opponents, the Bell System prohibited them from using Bell's lines. In practical terms, this meant that the farm companies would have to string their own wire if they wanted to connect their phones to those in the adjoining county. Knowing that these co-op companies had limited sources of capital, the Bell hoped that this ploy would effectively kill them off. It didn't. In fact, the

restriction on line use had the opposite effect; it forced the
small independents to band together for mutual survival. By
1900, the year in which the Bell Company officially began its
rural telephone program, the combined effect of low rates and
familism kept the Bell share of the rural market extremely
small. It has remained so. Although the Bell System provides
service to eighty-two percent of the available phone market
in this country, it has only thirty percent of the available territory and nearly all of it is in metropolitan areas.

We've come a long way (or have we?)

The independent telephone companies had to fight to stay
alive in their early years, and quite a few of the survivors are
still struggling. The service provided by the independents
runs from good to very poor. Mostly poor. This can be attributed to the fact that many of these small Telcos have never
really improved what they started with; in some cases, the
old crank phones are still being used. Conservatism plays a
large part in this failure to change with the times. Negligence
is also a factor. Those independent Telcos owned by firms
engaged in other types of business activities find themselves
with a low priority relative to the rest of the line. Take, for
example, General Telephone & Electronics, largest of the independents with eleven million phones scattered across the
country.

G. T. E. provides fairly good service in its larger service
areas and spends untold thousands on research for development of new products. But in Alabama, a banker complained
that he had to drive nearly thirty miles to another phone company's territory to place long-distance calls. It is all well and
good that G. T. E. has developed effective methods to catch
obscene callers, but wouldn't the Alabama banker be pleased
if G. T. E. built fewer Sylvania televisions and made his
phone work better instead?

United Telecommunications is the telephone company to
three million people. A subsidiary, United Business Communications, sells telephone equipment in Bell territory and
twenty-three other subsidiaries are engaged in all phases of

communications, from manufacturing to computer time-sharing. What must United customers think if they knew that the corporate headquarters of the United Utilities is using Bell equipment?

The Continental Telephone Corporation, the third largest independent company in the nation, gobbles up small co-op phone organizations as fast as it can find them. That makes truly impressive reading in its annual report, but customers in the areas acquired aren't impressed by annual reports. They want good service, and in some areas they don't receive it. In a Missouri rate-increase hearing, dozens of customers complained of noises on the line, inability to get anything but dial tones when trying to place calls, having to call forty miles away to get word to a neighbor down the street, over-charges, and discourteous personnel. Such customers have a succinct two-word opinion of the "fastest-growing phone company" that might be embarrassing to Continental's management.

All the independents have service problems, and correcting them is sometimes impossible because of the capital requirements. A telephone company with working capital of $80 or $90 thousand can't afford to spend several million for any reason, least of all for a change in switching gear. It'll be a long time before ESS (Electronic Switching Systems) comes to some isolated areas, and the independents are hard pressed to satisfy their customers in the meantime. There are ways of passing the problem on, however.

Some small independents solve their problems by allowing themselves to be absorbed by larger telephone organizations. Quite often, the buyer gets more than just equipment. It gets refugees. Bell, United, Continental, and G. T. E. phone offices are filled with forgotten middle-management executives whose sole qualification for their present position is an ancestor who founded the first rural telephone exchange and made it an heirloom. Buyers and sellers alike often feed the populace of an about-to-be-acquired area wondrous tales of the Telephone Utopia they will soon be living in, only to renege on these promises once the deal is consummated. In one southern state, the management of a locally owned Telco got up on the stage of the high school gym, along with representatives of the buying firm, and gave speeches and slide presentations illustrating how wonderful service was going to be shortly after the buyer took over. That was in 1969. In 1974 the service improvements had yet to be made. Complaints to the state regulatory board have met with scant success. The new phone company is still showing slides and making speeches. The regulators advise the complainants to be patient. The company swears it will make improvements before 1980. . . . Where will it all end?

The independents will continue to be plagued by service problems as long as they exist in their present form. But as the smaller companies disappear through acquisition, merger, or bankruptcy, the larger companies will take up their burden and hopefully eradicate the problems they inherit. Eventually, when all the acquiring and merging is finished—if only because there is nothing left to obtain—service will improve as the companies use available capital for improvements instead of invasions. Then Theodore Vail's dream of "One Policy, Universal Service" might come true as well. For, as service needs and capital requirements expand beyond the reach of all but the largest company, the "One System" goal announced a hundred years ago may become a reality.

The Family Structure

The people and machines that make up the Phone Company are organized to function in an army-like system. Indeed, more persons are employed by the Phone Company than fought with the U. S. Army in Europe in 1944-45. And, like the army, although the Telephone Company is designed for optimum efficiency the system often falls short of what everyone had in mind.

The similarities between the organization of the Telephone Company and the army chain of command are inescapable. From the way it is organized to the privileges of rank, the only thing missing is olive drab paint—which Bell stopped using in 1968.

From the group up

At the bottom of the totem pole is the "group," consisting of three to ten people, usually nonmanagement. All everyday telephone business originates at this level and, in all probability, the people in the group can do their job blindfolded because the work is mundane, repetitive, and dull. The group members make few decisions on their own. If the answer isn't written down or part of standard operating procedure, the members of the group must take the problem to their supervisor. (In the traffic department, however, there is an intermediate level—that of service assistant—who is responsible for deciding who can go to the restroom and when.) The members of the group are given vaguely descriptive titles, but these classifications—known as "net credited service levels"—are for payroll purposes only. It is not difficult to find a one-year man doing a job that's supposed to require five years' experience. The Bell System takes this yet one step further. It assigns titles to the group people that, aside from indicating pay levels, supposedly designate competency. But these job titles mean relatively little, as do grades E-1, E-2, and E-3 in the services. If you can endure, you are insured "promotion" to the higher level. Once you arrive at the top of your heap, however, the pay increases stop unless you make it to management.

Telephone Company management titles can be deceiving. Titles can mean everything or nothing at all.

The "first-line" managerial level includes secretaries, group supervisors, engineering staff people, and the floor maintenance man. These people file reports on group production, handle small problems—they can't hire or fire—and tell their supervisors in the most easily understandable terms what is going on in the "pits." The first-line supervisors are actually nothing more than people who receive higher pay than the other members of the group for doing the same work. Even the Phone Company realizes that someone has to be responsible for what's happening. The salary they receive is commensurate with the number of people who report to them and how much they make, which can make for some interesting discrepancies. Under normal circumstances, a Communications Marketing Manager with five people reporting to him makes less than a Business Office Supervisor who has seven people reporting to her. However, if two Business Office employees should switch departments, the salaries would reverse. It's a crazy, mystical formula no one is sure of except the payroll supervisors. About all that has been made public is that the salary range for first-line managers is from $13,500 to $24,000 a year. Since first-line managers must make at least fifteen percent more a year than their highest-paid underlings, the starting place on this scale can vary—and even rise and fall—depending on how much shifting of occupational employees is done below them. It can't fall too far since the median wage for nonmanagement Telco employees is $10,750 a year.

Above first line is a dimensionless void where people who aren't yet ready for the more responsible positions reside. People in this group can be recognized by a special title, the absence of people to be supervised, and general confusion about what they are supposed to be doing. While they report to someone, no one reports to them. They might advise but they never dictate. Here you find trainers, staff people, and special projects men. You can tell if they are going up or coming down by the amount of work they do. Not much work means they have been marked for corporate execution.

Several first-line managers and perhaps a few special project men will report to second-line managers. The differences between first and second line are so pronounced that you get the feeling from their attitude and the trappings of their job that these second-liners probably assumed their duties after receiving a commission from Congress. Second line marks the point at which management completely loses touch with the people doing the work. Seldom, if ever, will a second-line person converse with group members about anything having to do with Phone Company operations—this is the job of the first-line people. To bring to second line's attention those things that need attention is also first line's job. For deigning to listen, second-line people receive up to $35,000 a year.

As many as twenty group managers and ten second-line

men will report to the third-line manager. These people can have responsibility for a pretty fair-sized piece of ground, sometimes the size of Texas. Third-line people have the authority to do practically anything that needs doing. If a problem can't be solved on the third level, you can be sure that it involves at least a few thousand dollars and somebody's job. Third-line management, usually a district-level position, has a salary in the neighborhood of $48,000 a year.

Above third line, things start to get slightly fuzzy; titles are thrown around like confetti. There are defined areas, though. There is a division level, which takes in several districts. A general level, which takes in everything in an area that can be larger than a state. General managers make at least $65,000 a year and report to a vice-president and general manager (both terms taken together) who makes about $85,000 a year. V. P.s report to company presidents, who, in the Bell System anyway, receive the respectable salary of $150,000 a year for reporting to A. T. & T. Few people in the phone business make more than the president and chairman of the board of A. T. & T., who made $400,000 last year. If the dividend rate remains on par with previous performance, he'll probably get an annual salary increase that is twice as much as the yearly pay of an occupational employee who, by making the company work, ensures the level of the dividend.

Absurd status trappings go with these jobs. The group workers sit in a large room with a green and gray color scheme. The groups are arranged in little clusters and each metal desk looks like every other metal desk. In fact, if it were not for the black plastic name tags with adhesive backs stuck to the corner of each desk, everyone might get lost. Each group person has a swivel chair with a metal-rod back support with no armrests, and their desks are organized according to standard desk-organization charts. They each have a six-button telephone—green—with four buttons unused. For writing, they use Bell System property Bic M-39 pens. . . .

Group supervisors have little metal panel-and-glass pods to work in, also in a green and gray theme. They have desks identical to those used by their occupational people, but their chairs have armrests and their name tags, made of metal, are designed to be either suspended from the top of their partition or set upon the edge of the desk. Each group supervisor is also given a plain rectangular table to keep his books on and several straight-backed chairs for guests to sit in. His phone is a call director with every employee's line on it. It, too, is green. The group supervisor may use an olive drab desk pen with attached memo pad if he chooses.

Along the wall are glass and paneled offices with real doors to ensure privacy. In one of these the second-line manager performs those tasks required of him. He has beige furniture, a beige rubber strip around his metal desk, a padded chair, and a speaker-phone attached to his beige call director. He also has a beige metal bookcase and a desk-high metal shelf for important papers. His metal name tag, triangular to sit flat on the desk, has white sunken lettering on a beige field. His pen and pencil set is made by Sheaffer and comes in black or white plastic.

On the floor above, several secretaries sit in an anteroom guarding two massive oak doors. This is the office area of the district managers. Because they are management, the secretaries are entitled to furniture like that of second-line managers. They do not have a speaker-phone attached to their call directors, but they do have a small transistor radio for their listening enjoyment, which would be contraband for the troops below.

The offices they guard are impressive, to say the least. The theme is blue and Formica with few frills. There is a thinly cushioned couch for visitors, facing the darkly varnished wood-grained desk. A silver embossed name plate identifies the district man, who has a high-backed chair that can easily be turned for access to the Formica workshelf behind the desk. In the corner is a hat rack. The call director is beige with a speaker-phone. The pen and pencil set looks as if it is made of expensive wood. Closer inspection reveals it to be plastic.

Over in the area office, the secretaries have real offices for themselves. Done in standard second-line decor, the only noticeable addition is a standard issue coffee-maker. . . .

The office of the man they work for is a more sophisticated version of the district offices, with the name in gold lettering on the door. Still in blue and Formica, black naugahide has been added for that impressive touch. Also a closet is available for coats. The couch has more padding, the bookcase is higher, and there are personal touches—modern sculpture, a glass-topped coffee table, and framed diplomas. The call director is blue and so is the speaker-phone. The pen and pencil set is 14-carat gold with a white plastic inlay of the company emblem.

The departments

In every Telephone Company there are people who perform the following functions. The departmentalization may not be as clearly defined in some companies as it is here, but somewhere, someone is doing these jobs. . . .

You're a businessman and your company needs phones. A marketing representative from your local Telco calls on you to "talk about communications" and before you realize what you've done, you've ordered a new telephone system. Fine. The verbal agreement, the signed contract, the questions, and the presentation all went smoothly, and you fully expect that within sixteen weeks you will have an up-to-date communications system to handle your every need.

The marketing man takes your order back to his office and begins writing out the order for the gear that will be needed. The writing of this equipment order can take several hours and a couple of reams of paper, because the Telephone Company does not write an order using simple logic. Instead of saying, in effect, "replace that equipment with this equipment," the Telco order process requires that every piece of equipment be accounted for, whether it is involved in the order or not. If you want to add one phone to the six already in place, common sense would suggest that you request another phone. Well, the Phone Company writes an order that says to take out six phones and put in seven—and they must be taken out and put back in one by one. After the order is written, six copies are made for distribution—one for every department involved. (Later some of these departments will make copies of these copies, but that is confusing and not really necessary to an understanding of what is going on.) The receipt of an order is never acknowledged by anyone, so there is a great margin for error already. But let's assume that everyone gets his copy; now everyone involved knows that he should get ready for action.

The original handwritten order goes to the Commercial Department where it is checked for errors, typed, and entered into the order computer. Once this is done, six typewritten copies will confirm the order and let everyone know that Marketing is not just playing jokes. Commercial will keep its typed copy in the customer market file on your service rep's desk for future reference, should you discover that what you received was not what you ordered. . . .

The second copy of the typewritten order goes to the Traffic Department for assignment of trunk numbers, and to make sure that your equipment is not going to overload the circuits in your area. The Traffic Department will also send someone out to train your employees in the use of the equipment, an essential step nowadays. The Traffic Department also has operators on duty to help you during the trying days ahead.

Engineering uses its copy to design the electrical network that will take the system from your equipment room to the central office handling your exchange. Every one of the circuits has numbers, and every wire involved must be accounted for so that Plant doesn't wire your phones into the phone system of the company on the floor above you. The engineering work sheets, called circuit layout cards, are sent to the other departments. The reason it is done this way is because every department needs layout cards before anything can be done. Traffic needs the circuit numbers so that the circuits in your system won't be given to the retail store down the street, Commercial needs the numbers for reference, Plant needs the numbers for unknown reasons since it does everything by color codes, and Marketing has no idea why Engineering sends it a copy. . . .

Plant receives a copy of the layout cards, two copies of the order, and, ordinarily, several calls from the Marketing representative wanting to know why no one has ordered anything from the equipment supplier yet. The Plant foreman tells the Marketing rep that there is plenty of time for ordering and files the customer order away in a calendar file that he checks periodically. It takes one week for everyone to get a copy of everything. The Plant foreman gives his crews a week to put the system in once they get started, but before they begin work the order could stay in the calendar file in the Plant foreman's desk for as long as fourteen weeks.

The last department to get the order is Accounting, which uses its copy of everything to calculate the bill. When the system is installed—and even if it isn't because no one ever bothers to call Accounting when things don't go according to plan—Accounting will enter the billing information into its computer and start billing you from the day the equipment is supposed to be installed. Accounting also bills one month in advance, which is why you can't understand your phone bill if you receive it soon after the phone crews have been there. You were expecting to be billed for the installation, but not for the month ahead as well.

And so, about sixteen weeks after you placed the order, the Plant crews will show up and begin installing your phone system. The Traffic instructors will be teaching your people how to dial numbers, the Marketing rep will be running around excusing and soothing—to say nothing of softening the general mood of outrage—and the Commercial representative will be on the phone trying to find out why you got forty red trimlines instead of forty green call directors.

Policy

Now we will look at the Phone Company from its point of view. We will find out what it thinks about its customers, its employees, and other telephone companies. Then we will see what enables the Phone Company to act the way it does and get away with it. . . .

Customer policy

There *was* a time in our history when you could take Phone Company courtesy for granted. Nobody was astonished when you called the operator and she was courteous. When you called directory assistance, the operator was fast—but not so fast that she wasn't friendly and helpful. The installers were competent, the service reps were cheery—even when you were irate—and you could set your watch by the company's word; at that time, its word was its bond and it acted like it. Now all that has changed.

Official policy and actual practice still agree that everyone *should* be treated courteously and fairly—in the beginning at least. Beyond this point, the two never meet. Customers calling in with extraordinary problems and put on "hold" are referred to as turkeys, idiots, motherfuckers, and whatever other expletive can be hurled across the room in less than half a second. (If, by mistake, they haven't been put on "hold," other interesting problems arise.) People on the firing line in the Telephone Company tend to work under the assumption that you know exactly what you want when you make an inquiry, or at least that you know what the problem is. Many of these people expect you to know their terminology and get irritated when it becomes apparent that you don't. Yet these same people, when faced with the problem of giving you an explanation for what went wrong, turn this principle around and deliberately bewilder you with technical phraseology you can't follow the thread of, much less comprehend.

Phone people also hide behind the tariff—their bible—which contains rates, equipment descriptions, and, in some cases, governing policies. What makes it confusing—even to telephone people—is that it can be (and often is) ambiguous when it comes to setting down policy. It is not uncommon to find whole groups of telephone employees working under a wrong assumption in regard to tariff descriptions. A good case in point is what happened in Kansas City to WATS[1] customers.

---

1. Wide Area Telephone Service

Several WATS customers there wanted WATS lines in one place and extensions of those same WATS lines in others, which was all right since the tariff says you can have extensions of WATS lines in "off premises locations."

According to the tariff, there was a $7.50 monthly fee, plus mileage charges, for each extension, *when the extension was installed in another exchange area. This* was the problem.

One interpretation of the policy held that since Kansas City was an exchange, any WATS extension situated *inside the* K. C. *area* (several thousand square miles) could be installed for $7.50 a month, period. Six WATS extensions were installed under *this* tariff interpretation.

Another tariff translation held that an exchange was limited to an area with the same three-digit prefix. If the WATS extension was located *in another prefix area,* the mileage charge applied. Eight WATS extensions were installed under *this* interpretation.

The third, and last, concept of this involved tariff dictum had to do with the way Kansas City telephone exchanges were set up. Kansas City telephone areas are organized like an archery target with three rings. In this instance, each ring was considered to be an exchange area. More than ten WATS extensions were installed in the belief that if the extension was *in the same ring* as the WATS line, *no* mileage charge applied. This meant that the WATS line might be situated in the north half of the circle and the extension in the south. And even though the as-the-crow-flies mileage might be as much as fifty miles, no mileage charge was assessed because both were in what someone determined to be the same exchange area.

A company wanted a WATS extension in an adjoining exchange area, one that was in another ring. The Telephone Company, using concept number two, charged this company mileage even though its WATS extension involved a distance of no more than half a mile. Somebody finally figured out that everything was out of kilter and went to a higher authority for a definite decision on the matter—something no one else had bothered to do. The decision rendered held that of course

the second concept was correct, and that the other two were
so far out that someone should have known they couldn't be
right.

From that point on, all WATS extensions were installed
under the prefix-equals-an-exchange concept. But those installed under the previous misconceptions were never corrected. Many companies are still overpaying for their extension. But then, many of them are underpaying, so everything
balances out. . . .

The foregoing is an example of the way the people of the
Phone Company often interpret the tariff in their own way. If
they feel that your request may involve too much effort, they
might quiet you by saying, "The tariff doesn't allow it." If
they aren't sure of something, they ask you to let them "check
the tariff" and get back to you. When it looks as if they are
going to have to say no to your suggestion or request, and
they don't want to, they'll say, "Let me see what the tariff says
about this one." If there were no tariff, telephone people might
have to face up to situations that they would prefer not to. If
you get this tariff runaround, ask them to quote you the section, chapter, subject heading, and page number. Nine times
out of ten they won't be able to do it. If you want to see this
wonderbook, most libraries carry it. If you ask the phone people, they'll tell you that a copy is in the business office, knowing full well that most callers don't have the time to run
downtown just to look at a tariff, no matter how interesting it
may be.

Unfortunately, another factor with an important bearing
on how you are treated is knowing the right people. Great and
wonderful things can be done for you if you play golf with the
area manager every Sunday. One company in the Southwest
received a $1,000 credit it didn't deserve simply because the
president of this company went hunting every year with the
vice-president and general manager of the local Telephone
Company. Another company, with no golfing or hunting bud-
dies in the Phone Company hierarchy, had to pay $3,000 for
something even their Phone Company marketing representa-

tive felt was unfair. In the phone business, it's not who you are, but who you know, that counts. . . .

Even if you have compromising pictures of the Phone Company president, nothing can save you if you buy a phone system from an interconnect company.

If you tell a Phone Company rep that you are thinking of buying or leasing your own phone system, it will cause an awful sinking feeling in the area below his diaphragm. Within days the company will send out 90-caliber salesmen and consultants to talk with you, plead with you, and generally amaze you with the Phone Company's enthusiastic approach to "your communications problems." But if you withstand this heavy-handed company approach and buy a system from a competitor, everything comes to a screeching halt. From the day you start using alien equipment, your contacts with the Phone Company will consist of brief statements, curt answers, and evasive explanations.

If you turn in a service complaint about a scratchy connection, the company will acidly tell you that the problem probably originated in that foreign equipment on your premises and that they can't help you if you haven't checked with the "supplier who handles your system" yet. It's standard policy that the company will no longer originate contacts with you for any reason after you buy a system of your own. They will respond to your requests, but only grudgingly.

They will constantly remind you that most problems originate in outside equipment and that they therefore cannot be held responsible for any problems you might have. At every opportunity they will criticize the system you bought. Suddenly, billing errors are made and due dates are missed. Letters are "mislaid" and answered late. Installers profess ignorance and inability to do what you want them to. It's unbelievably petty, but it happens. Of course, if you want to get the Phone Company off your back and stop them from pestering you with pointless interviews, there is no better way to do it than to buy your own system.

There are many customer policy problems that have their

roots in the company itself. And if you got from your employer what phone people get from theirs, you'd take it out on your customers, too. . . .

Employee policy

In 1970, the Equal Employment Opportunity Commission, charging the Bell System with discriminatory employment practices, stated that the Bell System is, "without a doubt the largest oppressor of women workers in the United States." According to the EEOC complaint, women and minority employees of Ma Bell were losing an estimated $950 million yearly because of employment policies that kept them in low-paying and/or sex-segregated positions.

The statistics produced at that time were hard to argue with. Women held only 6.4 percent of the second-level-and-above management positions. In fact, the higher you looked the fewer women you saw. In ultrahigh managerial levels, women comprised only 2 percent of the total; this in spite of the fact that well over 58 percent of all employees were women. The EEOC report went on to say that the few women who did hold management positions were victimized no less than their below-deck occupational sisters. Salary ranges for all women lagged far behind those of men in the same positions. In 1974 women employed by Bell could expect to top out at $10,500 a year. For men, the top of the scale crested near $13,800.

The report also charged that women were effectively "cut off" from better-paying jobs by "job requirements" that affected nine out of ten standard occupational positions. The EEOC report stated that women filled 99.6 percent of the "operator" slots, 98.7 percent of the "service representative" positions, and more than four out of five of the clerical spots. At the same time, women held only 8 percent of the outside sales jobs and a miserable 1.1 percent of the available telephone craft positions.

Minorities fared even worse. Fewer than 12 percent of the one million Bell employees were non-WASP, which in itself was damning. But the EEOC went on to say that nine out of ten minority employees held positions on the lowest third of the wage scale—meaning annual salaries of $6,000 or less. In the ranks of management, minorities were all but nonexistent. Out of some 300,000 management positions available as of December, 1973, minority workers held fewer than 7,600.

For the defense, John W. Kingsbury of the Bell System told the EEOC hearings:

> In its zeal in trying this case against the Bell System, the EEOC has failed to recognize that the primary reason that the Bell System exists is to provide communications service to the American public, not merely to provide employment to all comers regardless of ability.

Notwithstanding that self-serving statement, he added that the Bell System was "fully committed" to equal opportunity employment and that Bell had been "unjustly maligned" by the EEOC.

Other Bell representatives tried to disprove the charges by inference. Claiming that one third of all managers were women, they were later forced to admit that their "management" category included such positions as secretary and service assistant. To fight the charge of "sex segregation" in certain jobs, the Bell staff claimed that men tended to be rude and obnoxious when in operator and service-rep positions—a hypothesis based on surveys taken in the 1880s. Furthermore, according to the Bell System, chairs, switchboards, and other "auxiliary" furnishings for operator maintenance were "designed expressly for women employees," and a change would be too much for either management to consider or the public to pay for.

Auxiliary furnishings, maybe, but chairs and switchboards?

Bell also claimed that there was a "considerable investment" in the image of operators as the "voice with a smile" and that a change to deeper, and supposedly grimmer, male voices would "inflict serious harm" on that promotional venture. Not exactly the kind of counterclaim the EEOC had in mind, but a noble try nonetheless. Its effectiveness was considerably weakened by the revelation that Bell had not used the "voice with a smile" slogan for two years.

By October 1972, Bell had decided to give ground. This decision was not based on the rightness of the EEOC charge, nor was it in recognition of Bell's failure to do what the government had made mandatory back in 1965 through the Civil Rights Act. It was a decision based on the cold, hard fact that Bell would never get another interstate rate increase from the FCC if it did not comply. As has happened so many times in the past, Bell showed that it could move mountains for a buck.

On January 18, 1973, in the U. S. District Court of Philadelphia, an agreement was reached that would get Bell off the hook. The Affirmative Action Program drawn up by Bell was accepted by the Office of Federal Contract Compliance and the EEOC, with reservations: these two government watchdogs insisted on reviewing the program every year.

Bell agreed to immediately give $38 million in back wages to employees who had been held back through job discrimination. It also agreed to give accelerated promotions and immediate wage increases to some 36,000 women and minority employees, at an estimated cost of $23 million. Bell also promised to eliminate sex discrimination by hiring men to fill 10 percent of the available operator positions and 25 percent of the clerical positions. In return, the EEOC stated that it was prepared to drop all charges.

By spring things were back to normal and Bell received its hoped-for rate increase.

One has to wonder about the effectiveness of the Affirmative Action Program. According to its 1973 year-end statement, minority management levels were still below 5 percent and women's share in management actually had dropped to 28 percent. The company's ads, claiming that 25 percent of all new Bell employees are from minority groups, sound impressive. But increases in Bell's total work force climbed less than 1 percent last year, and most new employees go into operator and service-rep positions, which, because they lack glamour and excitement, have a turnover approaching 60 percent a year.

It is perhaps significant, in light of the Affirmative Action Program and Bell's own avowed aims, to consider that, at this writing, women and other minorities—who together make up 62 percent of Bell's work force—had only one woman and one black man on the nineteen-member board of directors of A. T. & T. The other seventeen might just as well have come in on the boat from England.

If management undervalues its employees, then that is a reflection on the company. But when the people deny themselves the means of taking effective action by enduring the bumbling excesses of a union, then that is the fault of the people. There are few unions operating in this country with the inherent disdain for its membership demonstrated by the Communications Workers of America. Although it is the twelfth largest union in the United States, dollar for dollar it gives its members less than almost any other, and its size in no way reflects its popularity. Nearly all nonmanagement telephone employees have no choice but to belong to it and pay dues to it. The strike of 1971 made sure of that.

In the spring of that year, the C. W. A. began rallying workers to its cause by demanding 30 percent across-the-board wage increases for nonmanagement personnel. Vowing not to betray the trust of its loyal members, the C. W. A. presented a picture of grim determination: it was ready to call a strike that would last until the company gave in to its major demands, however long that took. Union publications also made mention of such things as dental care, cost-of-living wage increases, urban pay allowances, and wage scale reductions, but the big thing was that 30 percent wage increase—or so everybody thought. What many of the inspiring union tracts failed to mention was that the C. W. A. wanted a union shop where it could get it and an associated shop where state law permitted it, as well as the exclusive right to represent all telephone workers in those few enlightened states where union protection rackets were outlawed. It is a paradox of that place and time that those things wanted most were publicized least.

On July 19, 1971, the union rank and file walked off their jobs and took up picket positions around every telephone building they could find. Pamphlets and placards demanding that 30 percent wage increase were waved from every bastion. Many of these were handed out and carried by people ready to sit it out forever, should that be necessary. Everyone remarked on how serious this strike seemed to be, as compared with the previous one in 1968.

A week later everyone was back on the job. The union got a union shop where it wanted it, an associated shop where state law permitted it, and the exclusive right to represent all telephone workers in those few states that outlawed union protection rackets. The union did not get that across-the-board 30 percent wage increase. The union, happy with what it got, compromised—the rank and file would get 12 percent instead.

A revolution started almost immediately. Angry New York telephone craftsmen refused to abide by the union decision, and so did many other locals scattered throughout the country—they stayed out. And lots of envious—and angry—people began asking questions like: "Was the contract printed and ready for distribution before the strike was called?"

Few organizations can type copy, do layout, print 500,000 pieces of literature and mail them to a select nationwide audience in two weeks. But if the C. W. A. was to be believed, that's what had happened.

Hundreds of hushed little conferences were held all across the United States. Cajoling, pleas, and to a lesser degree, threats managed to bring 99 percent of the dissenters back into the fold. But the New York plant people responded to none of these. They would stay out until the following February before finally giving in to company obstinacy and union indifference.

While the union must bear full responsibility for the shabby handling of strikes in progress, part of the reason it never gets what it wants is due to the unique structure of the company—for few companies are so overmanaged as the Phone Company.

According to one observer, the Phone Company works under a reverse form of the Peter Principle; people of sub-par ability are promoted to high levels of management, where they struggle along incompetently until a strike rolls around. Then everyone reverts to his real level of competency to help the company pull through the crisis. Some people think the Phone Company has too many chiefs and not enough Indians simply because it just naturally grew into an oversized bureaucracy smothered in red tape. Others feel that the situation was planned to mousetrap the union.

Either way, the ratio of management to nonmanagement is 1 to 2.7, which hardly puts management in the thin-red-line category.

Promotions criteria are, at best, vague; at worst, scandalous. It is not hard to find examples of sexist promotion (giving bed-hoppers rewards for services rendered, by way of superfluous management positions) or pacification promotion (giving people bigger titles if they'll keep scandals quiet). While most personnel people agree that you should give someone a chance in a bigger job if he or she looks like 50 percent of what you're after, the Phone Company is willing to take a chance on you if you show a solid 25 percent. In any given phone organization, the chances of attaining at least a first-level management position are one in four. As one personnel supervisor said, "If you can maintain a 3.5 (on a scale of 4) profile consistently, and you are not a known sex offender, there is no reason why you shouldn't make management in five years."

The company has promoted people to first line in less than two years in some instances. In the bigger companies, an almost sure path to management lies in local union work. Since the companies fear a strong union, they are inclined to promote active union people just to keep the masses from having a strong leader to revolt under. After the EEOC stuck its head into Phone Company affairs, vocal members of women's and minority groups were given quick promotions in order to muzzle them. "This business makes no sense," the same personnel supervisor observed. "If you're qualified, they can't afford to promote you. So they end up with good-looking women, semi-revolutionaries, and the second or third best workers in their management slots."

Another sure-fire way to reach the gilded halls of the Phone Company is to get a degree—any degree. The personnel chief I talked with told me that his department once courted and eventually won the heart of a man who had a Master's degree. They offered him a fantastic salary and all but put it on paper that he would get the first second-line slot available. "The son of a bitch was a music major," the personnel man said. "We paid him all that money, spent a bundle training him, and gave him a second-line job within two months after he went to work for us. Six months after he started, he gave it up to go with the road company of *Mame*."

But if a college graduate decides to make the Phone Company his life's work, he can expect to be well taken care of. Stock purchase plans, low-interest loans, full hospitalization and life insurance, and company cars, not to mention a reasonable salary, make the Phone Company a veritable utopia for the security-minded individual who fears going out on his own. If there is even the remotest possibility of reaching the top, he can be sure it will go to the married-to-the-company man and not to some hotshot outsider. It always has been that way and it always will be. The top twenty-one Bell executives average better than 35 years with the company; as of last year, every one of the top 125 Western Electric people had started within the company and have known no other employer.

Bell is considerably worse than the other companies in this respect. In its 100 years, you can count on the fingers of one hand the company presidents who didn't start and spend their entire working life within the company. Unlike other industries, whose presidents often come in from the outside world to give fresh viewpoints and purposes to the business, Bell insists that it is better off as it is. It doesn't want to see itself as others see it—that would be too uncomfortable; that could rock the boat. If Mr. Vail were to return to his post after all these years, he would find procedures and practices virtually unchanged from the way he left them. Phone Company dogma has always held that you should change only when necessary and then as little as possible. This is the way management manages, and this is the policy that guides the troops.

Family Relations

The company that rides roughshod over its employees and customers cannot be expected to behave differently toward its competitors or regulators.

The F. C. C. offices occupy two floors in the Postal Department Building in Washington, D. C., and there its commission members meet once a week to determine policies that will affect the television programs we watch, the radio broadcasts we listen to, the satellite transmissions we monitor, and the amount we will pay the Phone Company to travel by long distance and stay a while.

You would think that there would be constant activity in a place where such vital things are determined, but there isn't. If you show up after lunch on the one day a week they meet, chances are that you'll find an empty room. There is no mad flurry of activity there, partly because there aren't enough people to start a flurry even if they wanted to, and partly because most of the policies and determinations are made elsewhere. Like in the headquarters building of the Telephone Company.

The Federal Communications Commission, born of the Communications Act of 1934, has the responsibility of setting interstate telephone rates, making sure that the customer receives service at acceptable levels, and seeing that the Phone Company receives an equitable rate of return on its investment. The F. C. C. does the first with regularity, the second upon occasion, and the third with religious fervor.

While interstate rates rise every three years or so "to offset rising costs," the service customers receive seems to be sliding downhill. If you think service is good, try calling New

York City on a Monday morning, or Los Angeles or San Francisco or Chicago. If your call goes through, the banshee-like wail or the crackling may make it unintelligible. And if you think the company's rate of return is inadequate, remember that the Telephone Industry will add between $6 and $7 billion to its assets this year, regardless of service conditions and F. C. C. rulings.

In any confrontation between the F. C. C. and the Telephone Company, the Telco has a better than even chance of getting what it wants merely through sheer weight of numbers. In 1972 the F. C. C. had 1,662 employees and an annual operating budget of $28 million. Against this small group, Bell alone had a million people and $56 billion. In this age of high-pressure lobbying and statistical bluff, numbers still count.

The Phone Company also has procedure on its side. Against a staff of political appointees, the Telephone Company pits a legal force of well-paid and unusually articulate corporation attorneys. So gun-shy is the F. C. C. that it will accept—as gospel—facts and figures presented by the Telephone Company in cases relating to rates and regulations. While the Phone Company has run afoul of other government agencies on many occasions, the F. C. C. as a body has defied it on an average of less than once a year.

When it wants a rate increase, it is standard operating procedure for the Phone Company to use methods that can best be described as dubious. If the Phone Company wants a rate increase of $78 million to take effect in 24 months, it goes before the F. C. C. with a request for $135 million to take effect in 18 months. The F. C. C. will turn this request down and send the Telco back empty-handed, making the F. C. C. look good in the eyes of those who still think it's a regulatory agency. The company returns, this time requesting $95 million in rate increases effective in 20 months. Hearings are held and, in the midst of the battle, the company announces that its supplier has increased wholesale prices. It must, therefore, have an increase on rates to offset the higher costs. Now remember, most Telephone Companies large enough to come before the F. C. C. receive their supplies from wholly-owned subsidiaries. If the supplier raises the rates, it's only because the parent company wants it to do so. The F. C. C. knows this, but most of the public doesn't. The F. C. C. now determines that the Telephone Company can have an increase, but *only* in the amount of $78 million and *only* if it waits 24 months. The company moans, the F. C. C. receives new laurels for its shrewd bargaining, and the public gets it in the neck. Everybody comes out ahead in these charades except those footing the bill. It happens this way every three years in a never-ending cycle. Employees strike for higher wages, the company gives them higher wages, the suppliers increase their costs right on cue, and the F. C. C. grants a rate increase to meet these higher costs. The employees strike for a percentage of the take, and so it goes.

Dealings with other companies are no less honorable. The Phone Companies have to work together if they want to keep their rates of return equal to that of General Motors. It stands to reason that if your call is made in United Telephone territory and travels through Bell's Long Lines, an equal sharing of the loot between companies is in order. It stands to reason, but it isn't going to happen. Both sides will hedge on figures, lie about facts, and threaten the other party. Some of these fights—especially those that pit a Telco giant against a Telco midget—take months to settle and leave the caller with no idea of what he is to be charged. For while the rates are fixed, the exact proportion of the divvy is not, and no charge will appear on the customer bill until somebody releases the information to the accounting department. This happens shortly after the percentages are agreed to.

Another potential trouble spot has to do with traffic densities and pricing. On high-volume calling routes—such as between St. Louis and Chicago—per-unit prices are low. The companies, if more than one is involved, make less money per call, but more in total. On the other hand, low traffic-density routes—such as between Butte, Montana, and Casper, Wyoming—mean fewer calls made and fewer dollars taken in. Here, percentages and rates are hotly disputed. The little companies claim that their return should not suffer at the expense of the big companies and argue that money lost in one place is made up in another by the large Telco, while they suffer if they don't receive an equitable share on their home ground because they operate in no other area. The arguments are endless and so are the fights. Complete harmony occurs only during rate hearings. The little companies are limited to cheering from the sidelines at such times and they do so with great enthusiasm, for a Bell rate change can do wonders for their own profit-and-loss statement.

The big and little companies also agree on the subject of interconnect companies; the fewer there are, the better they like it. The phone industry looks upon the phone sellers as poor besotted cousins, best left alone and ignored. If this cousin should get unruly, then the best course of action is to step on him hard. Although no phone associations have been convicted of price fixing (mainly because they do it legally—phone rates are set by the regulatory agencies more or less at the company's leisure) there have been attempts to drive the interconnect companies out of business. The Telcos, whose in-fighting sometimes becomes embarrassing to watch, band together with the fervor of religious fanatics to defeat a common enemy. In several states, the Telcos have actually managed to have interconnect companies declared illegal—only to have the decision overruled in court. The interconnect companies have no illusions about their status in the phone business, but their share of the market is increasing by $350 million each year and, as members of the free enterprise system, they make sure that their products and services become better every year. It is unfortunate that the regulated companies cannot do as well. . . .

Public Relations and Policy

The Telephone Company actively supports community betterment programs, encourages employee participation in community functions, and is prominent in local charity drives. But, as with the arch villain of the silent movie serials, it's a front to hide its real intentions. The Telephone Company could never accomplish what it does on a national level without the strong foundation it has built on the local level.

In practically every major city, Telco employees can be found in the Jaycees, the Kiwanis, and the Lions. On a higher level, Telco executives sit on the boards of local corporations in the cities where they operate. (A good rule of thumb here is that the size of the company, and the influence it has on the community, will dictate the status of the phone executive on the board. Company managers and vice-presidents hardly ever direct anything smaller than a bank.) This practice not only serves to diffuse the image of the Telephone Company as a massive corporation, but also serves to get the message across in circles where it can do some good.

The Telephone Company is also very big on Savings Bonds and The United Fund. Not because of its vaunted boosterism, but because these are two of the most visible money rackets around. Both of these charities (with the low rate offered on series E, there is no other way to describe Savings Bonds) have to rank as the biggest ripoffs ever foisted on the employees of a company. They are virtually shoved down employees' throats by an overly enthusiastic management. In one Bell office, the employees were told that if they didn't contribute their General Manager would do so himself, in their names. Very few failed to respond to this latent threat, and management people did not need to be summoned.

Savings Bonds make the company look good in Washington, while United Fund accomplishes the same end on the local level. Many consumers are ready to forgive poor service if it appears that the perpetrator is a corporate drum-thumper and Our Lady of Mercy rolled into one.

Another way the Phone Company gets what it's after is through its legal arrangements. Except on a very high level, most Telephone Companies farm out their legal work to local law firms. This gives the Telcos optimum leverage on the local political scene since the firms they engage nearly always have political ties. It helps keep state lobbying costs down, but this is not to say the Company scrimps on lobbyist expenses. Upon occasion the company has been known to truck

supporters of its causes to and from state capitals (as it did in
Missouri and Kansas in 1972), pay their expenses, and flood
the galleries with employees to give the impression that their
cause is just.

As long as these activities are restricted to telephone-
related subjects, company antics are within bounds. It's
when employees start fooling around with moral issues—
even on a tacit basis—that the game is changed. Take, for example, Lulu and her battle with the forces of degeneracy. . . .

A medium-level manager for a large Phone Company, Lulu
lived her life by the credo of archconservatism, deeply opposed to busing, urban renewal, Carl Rowan, fluoridation of
water, Mike Royko, Zionism, and sex with the lights on. It
was the last of these that suddenly got Lulu interested in the
theater.

As an active participant in local causes, she and a group of
cronies (the word is more appropriate than you might imagine) were discussing the deplorable state of affairs in their
city.

They did have a point. The local murder rate was spiraling,
grand larceny and theft were approaching epidemic proportions, the drug problem was spreading at an alarming rate,
and the Mob was leaving messy corpses all over town. But
what got Lulu & Co. where they lived was the unbelievable
number of adult bookstores and moviehouses.

With enthusiasm, Lulu and friends organized a local group
dedicated to the elimination of smut, vice, and the lingerie
section of catalogs. They searched for local targets. City
councilmen always managed to be out of the office when they
called, the police referred them to other departments, and po-
liticos did a manful job of containing their mirth while Lulu
and crew described the problem as they saw it in graphic detail. But it took the road company of the play *Hair* to give the
group a purpose and a cause of truly exciting dimensions.

"Do you want to live through a rash of rapes?" When the
local bastions of virtue heard that filthy words and pageants
of sex were about to invade the city, every Bircher, Baptist,
and Bible-thumper in the area rushed to the defense of truth,

justice, and white American womanhood. They were responding in part to a scandal sheet printed on Phone Company presses. Meanwhile, caught up in the jargon of the New Theater, Lulu was busy reporting her findings on the play to the city council in an open session.

Lulu & Co. read her no-holds-barred report on the play. To her way of thinking, it made a shambles of everything she held dear. The "hypnotic beat" was sure to be the downfall of the impressionable, and the "Dionysian nihilism" of the whole thing appalled her. When Lulu & Co. left the podium, few of her listeners spoke or applauded. Not because they had been moved one way or the other, but because no one understood what she had said. Dionysian nihilism?

She appeared on local television and radio shows. She helped organize "pray-ins" timed to coincide with the play's five-day run. She even got a councilman to sponsor a resolution to ban such filth. Many of her activities were conducted during the day, when, presumably, medium-level managers of the Company were expected to be at work.

Lulu & Co. fought the proposed production right down to the wire. But when it became evident that her efforts were in vain and the play would actually open, she and the minions of virtue went home and barricaded their doors against all the rapists who were sure to roam the streets in mobs. In the hours preceding the opening, Lulu did not stir—partly because the show was going to go on in spite of her, and partly because her employer had finally told her to shut up. The Telephone Company had had its fill of this moral cause, and besides, too many people who felt Lulu had made an ass of herself knew that she was connected with the company. The play came and went, the bookstores remained open, and Lulu & Co. sank slowly in the west. It was two years before Lulu surfaced again. Just about the time everyone had forgotten the *Hair* debacle, Lulu became a very vocal opponent of the Equal Rights Amendment. . . .

Section II: RESIDENCE SERVICES

Seventy percent of the 135,000,000 telephones in the United States are either owned by or leased to ninety million subscribers known to the Phone Company as "residence accounts." From the mansions of Grosse Pointe and Mission Hills to the shanties of West Virginia and Arkansas, these phones sit on desks, hang on walls, dangle from ceilings, or lie buried in the floor. They buzz, beep, ring, chime, gong, and trip sirens. But they all have one thing in common: every one of them is readily accessible to the other 134,999,999. . . .

Placing the Call

The migrant farm worker in California can call the President by dialing (202) 456-1414. The attorney general of the United States can be reached at (202) 965-2900. The one hundred thirty-five million can even call those in other lands. If you have some juicy news that won't wait until your next appearance at the Court of St. James, call Queen Elizabeth in London at 930-4832. If you've got cramps and the doctor can't see you for several months, the Chief of Doctors in Timbuktu can be reached at Mali 38. Whether you want to talk with your brother in Colorado or your pen pal in Tasmania, all you have to do is dial—and hope the call goes through.

The reasons it might not are numerous. Downed cables a thousand miles away can leave your call stranded at the nearest relay point; dust on a selector can cause the call to go astray; sun spots play hell with satellite transmissions; and gophers can do an equally disruptive job while sharpening their teeth on buried conduit. If you hear a banshee-like wail, it could be because a repeater in the central office is malfunctioning or because an employee left a peanut butter sandwich on the shelf of the 4-A switcher.

But these are just a few of the reasons why your calls don't go through the way they are supposed to. In fact, many of the phone foulings are not to be pinned on gophers, sun spots, or dirt, no matter how hard the company tries to fix the blame on them. The famous New York City Phone Fiasco in 1969-70 came about as a result of a conflict between advanced technology and an unbelievably gigantic bureaucracy.

In 1889, a man with the improbable name of Almon B. Strowger invented a gizmo that he modestly called the Strowger switch. This switch eliminated the need for an operator in placing calls.[1] With only minor improvements, this switch is still used in many Telephone Company central offices today. The way it works is this: The telephone numbers are gathered into "banks" of a hundred numbers in ten rows of ten. When a call is made, the first three digits dialed route the call to the appropriate central office, the last four up into the proper number banks and rows. The selector arm of the switch climbs the bank until it reaches the correct level for the digit being processed—a dialed five takes the selector arm to the fifth level and so on. When all four digits of the number are located, the call goes through. While this type of switching—known as step-by-step—generally consumes less than four seconds, it is too slow by current standards. With the number of telephones in use increasing by ten million annually, the need to eliminate time-consuming step-by-step switching will soon become imperative. Already developed are much faster means of completing and routing calls, but the company argues that conversion requires large capital investments and that as long as present equipment does the job there is no need to change. In some areas of the

---

1. A great improvement over the way things were being done up to that point. But Mr. Strowger did not invent his switch because of any great love of science. As an undertaker in Kansas City during the wild and wooly 1880s, he knew that a fortune awaited the man who got to the bodies first. He suspected that central operators were tipping off his business competition and invented the switch to foil their efforts.

country the Phone Company expects to use step-by-step switching gear well into the next century. Nevertheless, more advanced switching systems are in use. In the newer central offices—those built since 1938—crossbar switching equipment can be found.

Crossbar switching differs from step-by-step in that more calls can be routed at the same time on the same number frame. Crossbar switching is easier to maintain, resulting in less line noise and interference, and is much faster than step-by-step. Crossbar switches work in much the same manner as an "Etch-a-Sketch" toy. There are horizontal and vertical bars all across the number bank. When a digit is dialed, the vertical bar swings across the frame until it makes contact with the appropriate horizontal bar. The only trouble is that crossbar switching is still not fast enough for the needs of the future. Although call completion time is much less than that of step-by-step, crossbar systems have a tendency to backlog calls during times of heavy use. Realizing that the whole system may eventually bog down and never recover, someone finally invented ESS.

ESS—Electronic Switching Systems—takes only a millisecond to route calls. In fact, ESS can handle as many as 100,000 calls per second should the need arise (it hasn't, yet). The first switching system fully compatible with pushbutton dialing and its accouterments, ESS has untapped potential that could possibly make it the Strowger switch of the twentieth century. ESS is expensive—which is why it isn't found everywhere—but there are advantages to it that far outweigh costs. For example, with ESS, people will one day be able to do their banking by phone, make charge account entries, and reroute calls to a predetermined phone number. Those locations served by ESS equipment can expect to enjoy these conveniences by the late 1970s, but like so many other Phone Company innovations it will take years before distribution reaches everyone. Because of the long-term investment associated with ESS, most localities will continue to rely on the old step-by-step and crossbar systems for a long time to come. When call volumes are heavy, and especially as call volumes rise in the future, these old switching systems may be expected to die without warning. A few already have, and many others are showing ominous symptoms.

Call a number and you get a rapid busy signal even though the line is open. The call doesn't go through, or you find yourself talking to someone you did not call. These are symptoms of a central-office heart attack. The cause? Too many calls being made at the same time—during national emergencies, severe storms, and even peak business periods in large cities. Telethons create disruptions of major proportions when the cause is popular enough. Contests requiring contestants to call a certain number can do it. Popular recorded messages such as Dial-a-Whore in Los Angeles, or the Time and Track Results in the East, have created their share of breakdowns as well.

The Telephone Company forecast engineer's duty is to inform the rest of the company what to expect one, two, five, or ten years from now in the way of usage, people, and growth. Those men and women who do the actual work do a very good job in coming up with realistic estimates. Frequently they are accurate within one or two percentage points. But when the conceptual thinkers get their hands on the forecast information, they begin to worry about what *their* leaders will see. While the underlings worry daily about such things as service and accuracy, the executive officers are kept up nights by the demons of expenses, shareholders' equities, and the all-powerful Rate of Return. The lowly forecast engineer may accurately predict a rate of growth at ten percent in a given area of the city. In layman's terms this ten percent means fifty thousand new customers, new cable, new central offices, more employees, and a redesigning of present circuit arrangements. In Phone Company executive terminology, this means less profit and more expense. Corporate officers prefer to see a "reinterpretation of the available data." In other words, "We can't have this spend, spend, spend attitude when we've got an annual report to get out this quarter." The result is that a figure is lowered here and a decimal point is moved there to improve the profit picture. The result is also less cable, fewer employees, no new building just now, and an extraordinary mess when the fifty thousand customers do show up as predicted, expecting phone service. The new arrivals put up with slow installations and all but nonexistent subsidiary services. They endure bad connections and scratchy lines. And the Phone Company has fifty thousand customers who need not have been infuriated had the company put service in front of profit. This, in a nutshell, is what happened to the subscribers of New York City in 1969-70. The Telephone Company found itself in a hole because of a 20 percent underestimate of growth. Profits stayed up, but overall service fell to a level approximately on par with that of an emerging African nation. What's frightening about the situation is that alarmingly similar symptoms are showing up in Chicago, Phoenix, Los Angeles, along the Florida Gold Coast, San Antonio, Houston, Dallas, Colorado Springs, and Atlanta. It might be happening in your city right now. All you have to do is wait for the symptoms to appear.

Deposits

The Telephone Company looks upon new resident subscribers as a necessary evil in the never-ending struggle to maintain an acceptable Rate of Return. The company has no hard and fast policy regarding new subscribers. But it has guidelines, and a lot of people are strangled by them.

As a new customer of the Phone Company—one who has never had service billed to your name before—the chances of your having to pay a deposit for service are extremely high. The only real question—how much will you have to pay—is a difficult question to answer because there is no set policy, at least not on paper, anyway.

Generally, the deposit is equal to one month's billing, but it might be more—possibly as much as one hundred dollars just for one phone. The amount does not reflect your past credit history so much as it does the mood of the person you talk to, where you live, and how you sound on the phone.

If, as a prospective customer, you were to call the Phone Company Business Office three times on the same day and speak with a different individual each time, the odds are that you would be given three different deposit estimates. If you give the phone person a different address each time, no chance is involved at all. The closer you live to the so-called poverty areas, the higher the amount of the deposit will be regardless of your occupation, credit record, or "the tone of your voice." Often the Phone Company asks for a deposit if you speak with any kind of accent. If you live in an "undesirable neighborhood," the chances that you will have to pay a deposit are seven in ten. If you reside in the suburbs, the odds drop to three in ten.

Even if you've had phone service before, the company may ask you for a deposit if you are recently divorced, a serviceman, a college student, a single woman, a construction laborer, a gas-station attendant, an ex-con, or involved in anything other than an eight-to-five job.

On the brighter side of the deposit issue, the Phone Company is providing an excellent way for people to make their money work for them. People who have money on deposit with the Phone Company draw six percent simple interest on the principal. Unfortunately, the interest and the principal are not refunded; they are credited to the final bill. No one ever tells the depositer how much interest was made; you've got to take their word for the end figure. While the company has the money, however, it can truthfully be said that not one dollar in the entire 60 billion is idle. Somewhere, the deposit you paid out is being used, whether it be in capital improvements, land speculation, or in new advertising campaigns designed to make you forget that a monopolistic cartel has been holding your money. Since the company never makes an investment at *less* than six percent, it makes a nice tidy sum on money that, in most cases, it had no business taking in the first place.

How does one go about getting good credit with the Phone Company? If you maintain a satisfactory payment record for twelve months, the Phone Factory bestows on you one of its famous "B" ratings. Few credit bureaus and even fewer banks check your Telephone Company rating, quite possibly because the Phone Company hands out "B" ratings faster than political handbills in an election year. John Dillinger had a "B." So did Clifford Irving, Bobby Baker, Billie Sol Estes, and the entire cast of Watergate.

Even if you have a "B" and have paid your phone bill on time for the past twenty years, you can lose your credit if you change the billing name on your phone. If you decide to put the phone in your wife's name, she may have to pay a deposit as a new customer. Likewise, if you decide to put the phone back in your name six months later, you may have to pay a deposit as a new customer. . . .

Billing

How many times have you said, "This month's phone bill is too high!"? Well, you're right, but you're using the wrong terminology. What you should say is, "Next month's phone bill is too high!" With its wonderful capacity for logic, the Phone Company bills you one month in advance for monthly service and anywhere up to three months behind for long distance calls. If you look at it from the company's standpoint, of course, the system does make sense. After all, there's always the possibility that you might die, skip the country, or go broke during the next thirty days, leaving the company out one month's billing. Ignore the fact that the company is holding up to six months' billing under the guise of a deposit; it might have to wait until your will is out of probate before it can collect the final month's bill. No one (except the Democrats during their 1968 convention) gets phone service without paying for it first. Besides, the books balance ever so nicely if the Phone Company has money at the first of the month instead of at the end of it.

And what about your books? Let's say that you made a few calls while on a business trip and charged them to your telephone credit card. While you and your company's accounting department sharpen pencils waiting for the bill to appear, the Phone Company is locked in a grim struggle with another company over who gets what share of the take. Only when this matter is settled will the calls appear on your bill—and this may take up to three months.

Have you ever wondered exactly what it is you pay for on your monthly bill? Certainly not just the telephone—which in fact may be the one thing you're *not* paying for. You pay for the line, lights, service, bells, long distance calls, and directory advertising, but you do not pay for the phone itself. It comes free.

The line—which you know as your telephone number—and general services, such as directory advertising and maintenance, appear under "monthly service." You pay for long distance calls and any work you had done (moving, adding, or subtracting a phone) under another charge—an O. C. C.—which is confusing even to the Telephone Company. "Other Charges and Credits" sounds simple enough, but the wording reads like a 1925 civil rights law in Alabama. "Service added which was not previously billed" is O. C. C. jargon for "You had a phone installed." "Service discontinued which was previously billed" is translated to mean "You had a phone taken out." Sometimes these legalistic phrases are preceded by the words "Charge for" or "Credit applied to," which means that you owe or are owed a fractional amount of the monthly rate. Here again, the Phone Company doesn't tell you how it computes this fraction, and unfortunately, the O. C. C. is sometimes wrong. If you have the misfortune to receive an O. C. C., call the Phone Company and ask them to explain it to you. At best, you'll spend an hour listening to some poor devil discoursing on something he knows nothing about.

Explanations of your phone bill are hard to come by. Service reps and other company employees who are stuck with this sorry task usually try desperately to find reasons to delay giving logical explanations to problems even they can't understand. If an irrefutable discrepancy is uncovered, they do their best to do something about it, but the general unwritten rule on the subject is that if it isn't explained now, it won't have to be covered up later. If you really do need an explanation, ask for the monthly rates on every piece of telephone equipment you have—as if you were thinking about having the items installed. Get a firm rate for everything and work your way back from there. It's the easiest way, but you should exercise caution. The employees on the other end are experts in the art of talking the customer into a higher-priced item. . . .

A Wide Selection to Choose From

In the late sixties, American Motors ran a series of ads showing the Jewish Mother inspecting her son's new car. "Look at all the opticals!" she exclaimed as she pushed the button that ejected her through the roof. They were very good commercials. The Telephone Company also could have used the old lady in its commercials for, whether you realize it or not, the Telephone Company has "opticals" too.

In addition to the standard black telephone and flat-rate residence line, the Telephone Company offers no fewer than 36 types of telephone sets and at least ten different types of line service to its customers. If you want a telephone to complement the room decor, it's as easy as calling your service rep. But if you want economical phone service, choose one of the less expensive models. You can cut your bill by as much as one half if you're knowledgeable, or raise it astronomically if you're not careful. The average sales spiel of a Telephone Company service rep would bring tears of pride to the hardened eye of a used-car salesman. By never mentioning cost, these silver-tongued devils can sell the high-priced spread every time.

In all fairness to the company, it should be noted that most individuals spend more time selecting a bunch of bananas in the grocery store than they do ordering their telephone service, which, on the average, will see them through the next seven years at a cost of $150 a year. But the fact remains that the Phone Factory is generally very reluctant to divulge all it should regarding the cost of the various types of service it provides. Of course, the person taking your telephone order will give you the monthly rate for any of the services if you specifically demand it, but because some types of service mean a substantial dollar saving for you, the service rep isn't about to mention them or the rates unless you all but point a gun at her head. It's not her fault—it's the training she is given.

For instance, in cities where customers have a choice of flat rate for all the calls they make in a month or measured service (where they pay on a per-call basis), the Phone Company will almost invariably try to sell the prospective customer on using the higher-priced flat-rate line. "I'm sorry, but we offer measured service only on two-party lines" is the stock answer to requests for the cheaper service, uttered so as to create an undeservedly poor impression of "the two-party line." The service reps don't mention that most people only make about 38 calls a month and that, in spite of its tarnished reputation, two-party service creates far less trouble than one would imagine. Since measured service actually has a flat rate for a given number of calls—usually forty—and since it only charges for additional calls at a rate of about six cents per call, 80 percent of residential telephone subscribers could save $70 a year by utilizing measured service. For its part, the Telephone Company bears the same maintenance expense for measured-service lines as for flat-rate lines, and its accounting costs are higher because records must be kept of the number of calls made on the measured line. If you make relatively few outgoing calls each month, it might be well worth your while to check into measured service. Of course, your saving depends on how much you spend per month on frills. You may not save a dime if you have a beautiful decorator phone in any one of eighteen gorgeous colors.

One of the more revolutionary developments in the Telephone Industry happened a few years back when the telephone sets suddenly ceased to be solely functional and became decorative as well. Today's telephones come in beige, blue, copper, gray, green, ivory, pink, red, turquoise, white, yellow, and black. And if none of these colors fits your needs, you can mix any two or order a special finish whipped up to your specifications, as long as you are willing to pay for it. Once you've decided you want a telephone the color of a robin's egg, you have only to pick the type of phone. Here the selection may not be as wide, but it is certainly no less interesting.

You can choose from phones that sit on desks, hang from the wall, lie on the floor, or are imbedded in, or dangle from, almost any part of your home. When you've made that decision, a door opens to a whole new area: Just exactly what is this baby-blue hanging phone going to have as standard equipment? Is is going to have a bell or a chime? A dial wheel or push buttons? Should it even *have* a dial wheel or push buttons? Should it be portable or fixed? Have a short straight cord or a long spring cord? If you hesitate to make decisions, the telephone selection process can be maddening. Especially if, in the first place, you just wanted a black telephone to sit in the hall. Phones today have night lights, they have the works in the handset, and some even resemble packages of tissue paper. But no one has yet been able-to make them so that they consistently get a dial tone. . . .

Decorator Phones (Outside Supplier)

Even before the days of wild competition, residence subscribers could get a phone from an outside supplier, but today the selection is wider than ever before. Everyone from Montgomery Ward to the Olde Antique Shoppe is selling telephones outright. If your aesthetic sense is offended by the crass plastic units offered by the Phone Company, you can purchase an elegant reproduction of a turn-of-the-century French *télécommunicat* from Penney's for about $45.

But as you walk out the door with your brand-new telephone tucked under your arm, don't get the idea that your phone bill is about to take a sudden plunge just because you've bought your own instrument. There probably won't be any noticeable decrease in your monthly bill and, almost inevitably, you're going to be hit with an O. C. C.—a sizeable inspection fee. Regardless of the pitch handed you by the salesman who sold you the new phone, the Telephone Company is going to make you pay through the nose for your alien equipment, which it can easily detect through voltage readings and other means.

The Bell System has a set policy—as do most of the other Phone Companies—stating that customer equipment must undergo an inspection to ensure its compatibility with Telephone Company equipment. Because there is an outside chance that your store-bought phone will blow all the circuits in the central office, the Company wants to check it out. Regardless of what it finds, the charge for this inspection *starts* at $35. No matter what the salesman told you or what appeared in the store's advertisement or what it says on the box about compatibility with Telephone Company equipment, the company has to check and inspect. If the company finds out on its own that you have a phone from the dime store, your service will be shut off.

In any event, you say, the inspection-correction procedure is a one-shot proposition. True, but that initial outlay isn't the half of it. If your company-provided service amounted to no more than a standard telephone and perhaps one or two extensions, the monthly rate for your new personalized telephone is still going to cost 80 to 90 percent of what you used to pay, because the company never billed you for the phone per se—they got you for the line, which still comes into your new telephone. Even the charge for push-button dialing is associated with the line and not the telephone. So while you may have the prettiest phone on the block, in the long run everyone else's is cheaper and probably will last a lot longer. Even if nothing else can be said about Phone Companies, their telephone sets might as well have been made to withstand a direct hit from a 105mm recoilless rifle. Anyway, the appeal of "antique telephones" lies in their appearance— they look just like the phone grandma had back in 1906. Recognizing the presence of this market, the Company has taken steps to keep it alive and thriving. The company now offers antique phones at a cost that's on par with the dime-store varieties. Although the selection isn't as wide, they work better—but only because the company's poorer-quality instruments have been bought up by outside suppliers.

Every now and then, the local Telephone Company will take pity on its rural subscribers and update the local phone equipment. They replace the old models with new (more expensive) models. Once the changeover is completed, the company doesn't destroy the old phones—it sells them. Enterprising hucksters buy these "antiques" by the gross and unload them on retail outlets that deal in Objects d'Americana. The first inkling the antique-hungry public has of these transactions is an ad buried in the classified section: "Antique phones. Found on a recent buying trip. Limited quantities available." Enticed by the ad, bargain hunters swoop down to get a darling telephone reeking of Christmas turkeys and grandmas with their hair in buns. The salesperson assures you that this phone will work like a charm if you know how to plug it in, and so you've bought yourself a phone that even the Telephone Company thinks is too old to remain in service. This phone is in the same condition it was in when the company men ripped it out of the wall, and when you plug it in your phone jack you're going to have the same problems the residents of Fairbanks, Iowa, had before modernization.

One-Time Charges, Long Cords, and Gongs

Until recently, the most ridiculous and unfair charge the Phone Company demanded was the one-time shot for colored telephones. In most localities, the color charge was five dollars. Period. The first red phone that you ordered during your lifetime cost five dollars. Every succeeding one— regardless of the color—came at no additional cost. You could change colors every week and never have to pay for color again.

According to the rate people, the color charge was not a direct reflection of the manufacturing cost. It cost no more to produce a green phone than a black one. No, the color charge applied because the company felt it ought to receive some financial remuneration for making pastel phones available to the masses. The color charge—which in its last years poured as much as $15 million annually into the company coffers— simply provided a nice source of revenue. No special care was needed to make or install them—they were and are no different from the black models. As early as 1969, a rate man freely admitted that the color charge was about to go the way of the crank phone because the company felt it had just about milked the color-hungry public dry. He knew what he was talking about. The color charge disappeared in 1972.

Akin to the color charge is the one-time long-cord charge. The charge is for cords of abnormal length, which might seem reasonable if the company had to order from the factory every time it needed one. But company warehouses are filled with cords of every imaginable length and hue. They are produced in bulk and in lengths of about twenty-five feet. If you order a thirteen-foot cord, the remaining twelve feet are cut into six-foot sections to fill other orders. In any event, you will pay upwards of four dollars for "long cords" and, here again, the charge applies only to the first long cord you order.

One of the more inane aspects of the long cords is the Indemnity Agreement required when you order a twenty-five-foot straight cord. The Indemnity Agreement releases the Phone Company from responsibility in the event that your cord strangles someone. If an individual trips and falls because of your telephone anaconda, it's your problem, not the Phone Company's. The Indemnity Agreement is required only with the twenty-five-foot straight cord. The thirteen-foot spring cord, which can be stretched to a length of better than twenty feet and which vibrates like a seismograph at the slightest touch, requires no such document.

Those of you who live in suburbia know the anguish of missing calls because you're out in the yard picking dandelions. If the thought of missed calls keeps you up nights, call the Phone Company and request the installation of an extension bell. The rate is nominal and you will never again miss hearing a call if you are anywhere within 200 yards of your phone. The ring of the extension bell is almost identical to the ring of the phone itself—except that the extension bell is all but capable of raising the dead.

If the extension bell seems a bit much for your sedate taste, order a gong. Gongs are especially in demand by those people who enjoy Japanese rock gardens or the opening scene of J. Arthur Rank motion pictures. The Telephone Company gongs make up for their lack of resonance with sheer volume, but they add a nice touch to anyone's incoming calls.

At the other end of the spectrum are the sedate dignified chimes, the poor man's answer to Big Ben. Every time a call comes in, a delicate tone summons you to the phone. However, some people have encountered problems with chimes after a while. And to hear them tell it, nothing upsets the digestive tract so much as Big Ben's melody half a note off key. . . .

The Numbers Racket

The most widely read book in this country is not the encyclopedia, the dictionary, the cookbook, Who's Who, The Boy Scout Manual, or even the Bible—it's the telephone directory. According to company statistics (one of the few it can be proud of), over 93,000,000 people used the Yellow Pages 3.6 billion times last year, and the White Pages figure isn't far behind that. Even though these figures are part of a gigantic sales campaign designed to sell Yellow Pages advertising, no one can dispute the fact that these two volumes provide fast and easy access to eighty million telephone customers.

Unfortunately, the telephone directory provides such easy access that the hapless people listed are constantly beset by calls from a horde of flim-flam men, gyp artists and perverts, to say nothing of sponging relatives, nosy neighbors, and the much-publicized teen-aged fanatics who have dedicated their lives to the idea of controlling all telephone circuits. To avoid calls such as these and for reasons of their own, about 9.5 million persons choose not to be listed. Even if their reasons are absurd, it seems logical that a bill-paying customer has a right not to be listed if he doesn't want to be. The Phone Company doesn't see things that way.

The company views nonlisted and nonpublished numbers as a distinct disadvantage to "good service." Reasons cited include:

> The inconvenience to family and friends, the risk of not being available during an emergency, and the general inaccessibility to any incoming calls. . . .[1]

---

1. Bell System publication, 1972.

From statements such as this and from ads of a similar nature, you'd think that the company had a genuine interest in your welfare. It does to a degree, of course, but the main reason the company frowns on nonpub and nonlist numbers is based purely on financial grounds.

It costs the Phone Company at least six thousand dollars a year to employ an operator in the larger cities. Equipment necessary for her to do her job also necessitates a large capital expenditure. In a city of 500,000 people, as many as two hundred operators are needed to man the information exchanges around the clock. Since the operators and their equipment aren't about to sit under a tree while doing their job, a building must be provided. The switchboards require space, as does the cable connecting the switchboards to the central office lines. Taken as a whole, directory assistance has never made a dime for the company. And although it is presumably paid for through the monthly service charge of each and every customer, the company can, upon demand, present figures to show that directory assistance is nothing but a constant dollar drain that lowers the Rate of Return and the yearly dividend. The Company states that it costs 7.1 cents to handle a directory assistance call, and it feels that every directory assistance call is time and money wasted. Why? Because everyone's telephone number ought to be listed in the directory, and anyone who wants to place a call ought to be intelligent enough to look up the number without the help of the company. The trouble is that a lot of people find it easier to call 411 than to go through the directory looking for "Smith, John E." on Elm Street. But the company has plans to stifle this sort of thing within a very few years by instituting a charge for calling directory assistance. In some locales, this charge may be as high as 25 cents.

The company already has taken steps to revenge themselves on people who wish to preserve their anonymity. In several large cities, the company charges a dollar per month to keep your name and address out of the public eye. The company feels that twelve dollars a year just about offsets the cost of all those directory assistance calls it must handle because you're not in the book.

A Snowball in Hell

In an organization the size of the Telephone Company, mistakes are bound to happen. What makes Phone Company errors more interesting than ordinary corporate errors is the number of them—and its obstinate insistence that such mistakes never happened in the first place. But here are documented instances of some that did:

1. In St. Louis, an elderly woman received her monthly bill and noticed that something was amiss—the bill was for $63,437.50. She called her service representative to point out what she considered to be a glaring mistake, certain that the situation would be quickly rectified. Her service rep pulled out the company copy of the bill to make sure that what she said was true. After the woman finished her story, the service rep suggested that she go ahead and pay the amount shown on her bill. *If the company found that there was indeed an error,* he told her, it would credit any overpayment to her account. Oddly enough, the lady protested. She was referred to the service rep's B. O. S.[1] Again she was told to pay. The woman declined. The company cut off her service. Two weeks later, the company sagely decided that it had indeed miscalculated. The lady received a new bill—for $63,400 less than the first one.

2. In Denver, three roommates came home to find a gaping hole where their wall phone had been. The girls called the police. After a week of exhaustive investigation, the police announced their findings: A former roommate of theirs had not paid her bill and the Phone Company computer, not realizing that she had moved, issued the necessary orders for the disconnect of the wrong phone. Case closed . . . almost. The company refused to believe that the felon was not living where their computer said she was and staunchly refused to put the phone back in. After signed affidavits were produced and legal action threatened, the company finally backed down. It was never explained how the company got into the double-bolted apartment in the first place without anyone knowing about it.

---

1. Business Office Supervisor

3. In San Diego, a man was certain that the $246 worth of calls to Ghent, Belgium, on his bill had not been made either by him or any member of his family. He brought this fact to the attention of the first Phone Company employee he talked with. Apparently, this was the wrong person. The charges reappeared the following month. Again he called. This time he was assured that the problem would be taken care of. It was. A week later he couldn't even call the house next to his, because the company cut off his service for nonpayment. Three weeks of threats, pleas, and coercion didn't change the situation at all. Then, suddenly, the phone started working again. No reason was ever given. No explanation was ever offered.

4. In Chicago, a woman ordered phone service for her new home. The order was taken, written, and distributed with only one minor error—a decimal point two digits to the right of where it should have been. The woman's first bill, excluding installation charges, was for $2,550. . . .

5. In Pittsburgh, a family moved across town and expected their phone to follow. It didn't, but the bill did. After they had called the company to try to get the phone they were paying for, the company installed one, but that phone was simply added to the bill for the phone they didn't have. After three months, the company called, demanding payment for the nonexistent phone the subscribers had refused to pay for. Once again, the problem was explained to the company's apparent satisfaction, but when the next bill came the family was still being charged for the phantom phone. After eight months the billing was stopped, but only after the company made one more attempt to collect the unpaid balance.

6. In Phoenix, through a billing error a deceased individual's phone bill continued to be forwarded to his next of kin for three months after he and the phone were disconnected. Because the subscriber himself had not been the one to notify the company, it insisted upon payment. His survivors refused, even when confronted with the company's wonderful logic: ". . . We cannot be expected to know when a

subscriber dies and wants his service discontinued. He should have called us before he died. . . ."

On occasion, the Phone Company allows itself to be led astray:

7. In Miami, a group of students wanting service had the service billed to their pet grouper. For three months the bill, addressed to S. E. Bass, went unpaid. When the company called, one of the clan suggested that the company representative call on Mr. Bass, to which he readily agreed. The meeting, scheduled to be held at the end of a long pier, failed to materialize—as did a subsequent meeting at Marineland. For six months, the collector wandered about the shoreline before someone noted that on the application for service Mr. Bass had listed his previous residence as the Gulf Stream and his present occupation as a mantelpiece. To the company's credit, it did not try to take Mr. Bass to court.

The monumental mistake is not a fluke of nature within the Phone Company. Errors such as these occur more often than anyone could imagine. Because of the large number of company employees who have contact with bills and orders for service, the magnitude of an error on any given account tends to snowball. A minor error at the source can go undetected through channels, gaining momentum until it is very large indeed. How many potential problems are there? It has been estimated by financial experts that as many as 90 percent of *all* telephone bills contain an error or mischarge. Although this figure seems much too high, the company's claim that 96 percent of their customers have error-free service is probably much too conservative. But even if the company's claim is accepted, it means that at least 3.6 million accounts are being misbilled every month. Yours could be one of them.

Push-button Melodies

One of the happy side effects of the telephone technological revolution is the new musical instrument, the push-button phone. Push-button dialing cuts dialing time, allows the transmission of high-speed data, reduces the chance of dialing errors (in the company's equipment, not yours), and offers unlimited possibilities for future uses. In addition, some budding Bach has found an entirely different use for the push-button phone. By careful experimentation, our unsung hero found that many melodies—or at least parts of melodies—can be tapped out on the ten-button and twelve-button models. Of course push-button phones were never meant (and therefore were not designed) to be used in playing the musical scale. At most there are only twelve notes and most compositions require more than twelve notes. But the *Push-button Telephone Songbook*, Vol. 1, by Michael Scheff, contains thirty-seven tunes that can be played in whole or in part on your push-button phone. One word of caution to all would-be musicians: be sure to call a friend—who can leave his phone off the hook—or a dead number first. If you immediately start playing your phone without first taking precautions, you may dial a long distance call to Santiago, Chile.

Long Distance Calls

Because long distance rates and practices are the same for both residence and business customers, a discussion of long distance services will appear in the business section.

Section III: RIPOFFS, ROBBERIES, BLUE BOXES, AND FRAUD

When Daniel Ellsberg published material that the government of Richard Nixon felt was detrimental to its well-being, it employed burglary, blackmail, threats, and coercion to try to stop him. Richard & Co. failed.

When Ramparts magazine published material that the Phone Company felt was detrimental to its well-being, it employed blackmail, threats, and coercion to halt publication. Bell & Co. succeeded.

A seemingly airtight case involving an alleged member of the underworld was thrown out of court when it was discovered that the wiretap order was signed by an assistant to the attorney general and not by the attorney general himself.

A Bell employee with nine years of service was fired, hounded, harassed, burglarized, and beaten, merely because he was overheard talking to a suspected phone phreak during what he assumed to be a private call.

Two teen-agers were caught breaking into the coin box of a pay phone. They received six-month prison sentences. The "take" in their heist was $73.40.

A coin supervisor was caught padding his pockets with nickles, dimes, and quarters collected by his people in the collection department of a midwestern Telephone Company. He admitted stealing more than $6,000 and was asked to resign. He did and no charges were filed. . . . .

Taking Care of the Customer

In an effort to "minimize tariff abuse," the company begins checking 20 percent of its one- and two-line customers every year by means of electronic surveillance. "It's nothing new," claims one phone executive. "We've been doing it for years."

"The confidentiality of customer records is sacrosanct." So testifies a regional manager of the Bell System. Yet his company, only three days later, confronts one of its business customers and orders him to cut back on the number of directory assistance calls he makes. As proof, the company shoves a computer printout sheet under his nose. On it is listed every directory assistance call he has made in the past two months, the numbers he called, how long he talked, the day and time. . . .

Although the company refuses to authorize records checks unless they are subpoenaed and cannot authorize wiretaps except on written authority of the attorney general of the United States, it successfully lobbied for a section of the Omnibus Crime Act of 1968 that enables it to "make random

81

checks to maintain the quality of service"—in other words, tapping lines wherever and whenever the company feels like it. Under the law, the company doesn't have to justify such actions to anyone. The act of surveillance is done in complete secrecy.

Well aware of its own rules regarding harassment of customers while collecting overdue accounts, service reps in a West Coast city are told to disconnect the customer's service if he refuses to be reasonable regarding the payment of his bill.

For making $30 worth of fraudulent credit card calls, a young Washington, D. C., college student is given a thirty-day jail term and fined $250. In that same city, a phone employee caught doing the same thing tells a plausible story and is merely suspended for three days and told not to do it again.

A bitter opponent of interconnection, Bell provides "statistics proving conclusively that interconnection causes 25 percent more repair problems." When asked to provide figures on its own repair problems, Bell refuses to do so.

The Ramparts Affair
". . . Bell's self-protective reflexes have created an atmosphere of fear that may well muzzle deserved criticism. . . ."[1]

The article scheduled to appear in the June, 1972, issue of *Ramparts* magazine was not innocuous. It was calculated to cause a run on the available copies. Although this is exactly what happened, the demand was not caused by the regular readership. It was created by a Phone Company anxiously trying to avert what it was sure would be a financial disaster.

The subject of the article was mute boxes and how to build them in 19 easy-to-follow steps, although you never would have known it had you not read the article itself. For the title, "Regulating the Phone Company in Your Home," gave hardly a clue to the material at hand. The two-paragraph lead-in attributed the information in the article to "documents which

---

1. *Business Week* Magazine, February 2, 1970.

have come into our hands," and no specific mention of the
subject matter appeared until the last sentence of the lead-in.
The body of the offending article was written in a style best
described as Early *Popular Electronics*, but if the directions
were followed to the letter the reader could build himself a
dandy little mute box. Although the article (or document) did
not specifically spell out the criminality involved in making
and using such a device, the last several paragraphs were devoted to ways and means of avoiding detection. Assuming
that you were intelligent enough to build the unit, you were
also supposedly smart enough to realize that there could be
penalties. *Ramparts* did not tell its readers about the $500 to
$1,000 fines and the year in prison awaiting those who were
caught. Even if this had been done, it is highly unlikely that
the Phone Company would have reacted any differently because the company saw no ground for compromise. The only
act that would assuage its passionate anger would be a mass
book burning. For all intents and purposes, the Phone Company got what it wanted.

It began on May 12, 1972, near the end of the working day.
A special agent of the Phone Company walked into the *Ramparts* office, gave the receptionist a sheaf of paper and his calling card, and left. The next morning, he called. The pile of
paper he left the night before was a copy of the California
Penal Code, he explained, and for the benefit of everyone concerned he had underlined a section sure to be of special interest. Section 502.7, covering the illegality of selling "plans or
instructions for any instrument, apparatus, or device intended to avoid telephone toll charges" and stating the penalties for doing so, merited attention. Having said all he intended to for the time being, the special agent hung up. The
threat, carefully veiled in the agent's well-modulated tone,
might well have impressed the Mafia.

It is fortunate for us that the initial threat failed to achieve
results. Had *Ramparts* backed down immediately, we never
would have known the extent of the company's rage—or the
extent of its power. The "*Ramparts* Affair" graphically illustrates the all-pervading influence of an organization in some

ways more powerful than the government. Only by exposing its corruptive influence can we see that something definitely needs to be done to remedy the situation.

The next step the company took was to notify the Associated Press that it intended to file civil charges against the magazine and criminal charges against the editors. This was by no means an empty threat. In San Francisco, where *Ramparts* is published, the company's legal staff numbered 160. These agents moved to block the distribution of the magazine.

Many copies had already been mailed to subscribers prior to the Phone Company's entry into the case. The company demanded access to the mailing list so that it could keep *everyone* listed under surveillance. *Ramparts* refused.

The Phone Company demanded that the copyright of the article be turned over to it to prevent anyone else from publishing the material. It also told *Ramparts* to answer reporters' queries on the matter with a curt "no comment." When an outraged publisher at first refused to concede, the company unleashed its big guns. It threatened 500 magazine distributors scattered all across the country. Under this serious economic threat, the publisher finally agreed to withdraw the June issue from the newsstands. The Phone Company now had only to worry about the one copy in five that reached the public through subscription sales and those that had already gone to the newsstands before the withdrawal order.

The company made an effort to recapture them all. Sending out agents in a nationwide move, the company covered every library and isolated newsstand it could find. In a memo, Bell directed its employees that the *Ramparts* article should be "collected by any means necessary to effect their removal from newsstands and magazine racks in public places," and that "the exact method for collection . . . will be left to the discretion of individual supervisors. . . ." Some supervisors made the order crystal clear: steal.

By now the publicity was such that a few radio stations had decided to read the story over the air. The Phone Company quickly cut them short with threats of criminal charges.

Perhaps the article wasn't an example of responsible jour-
nalism, but the subsequent suppression wasn't any kind of
example of freedom of the press, either. Simply because you
tell someone how a bank can be robbed does not make you
guilty of criminal conspiracy—especially if you are describing methods that have already been used. A prime example of
this is television scripting. An idea dreamed up by some
scriptwriter may influence a real-life criminal—it's happened
before and will happen again. But the scriptwriter cannot be
held responsible because some fool goes out and puts his idea
into actual practice. For the same reason, *Ramparts* should
not be held responsible for the possible actions of its
readers—or so you'd think. That *Ramparts* can be held responsible has already been established through good old section 502.7 of the California Penal Code. The author of section
502.7 freely admits that he sponsored the bill for the benefit of
several telephone lobbyists he partied with during several
sessions of the legislature.

While not a crisis of major proportions to anyone except
Ramparts and a paranoid company, the "*Ramparts* Affair"
clearly illustrates how far the company will go to protect its
interests within the business sector of its customers. But the
company is no respecter of individual rights, either. As we
have already seen, the Constitution is no great hindrance. . . .

The Blue-Box Gang

> In all Criminal prosecutions, the accused shall enjoy
> the right to a speedy and public trial, by an impartial
> jury of the state and district wherein the crime shall
> have been committed, which district shall have been
> previously ascertained by law, and to be informed of
> the nature and cause of the accusation; to be con-
> fronted with the witnesses against him; to have com-
> pulsory process for obtaining witnesses in his favor,
> and to have the assistance of counsel for his defense.[1]

---

1. The Constitution of the United States, Article Six, para. 1.

His name is not important. What happened to him is.

Since 1962, his employer had been Bell and, in the nine years he was with them, he worked his way up to a position of responsibility as coordinator between Bell and Western Electric. In his spare time, he was a radio officer for a civil defense unit and a well-known electronics enthusiast. His employer was satisfied with his work and he was satisfied with his employer. Things couldn't have been nicer.

One night he met another electronics buff. They talked about things of mutual interest and, after mentioning that he worked for Bell, his new-found friend asked him if he was familiar with phone phreaks and their activities. He wasn't, so his friend filled him in. He couldn't believe the things he was told. His new friend set out to show him that what he said was true.

This friend was already under surveillance for his phone-phreak activities. When he called our man to innocently ask about car telephone units, the security men listening in thought the two men were discussing portable blue boxes. Based on what was overheard, the security staff immediately marked their fellow employee as a spy and turncoat. Although he didn't know it, nearly everything he did and nearly everything he said was monitored from that moment on.

One night, his friend gave him a phone number to call to prove that phone phreaking really did exist. What he heard appalled him. He immediately did what any good employee should—he called security. Security asked him what he thought they could do about it and hung up. He was soon to find out.

A few hours later, two security men and a local policeman showed up at his home and began searching the premises. Although neither of the Bell men was named on the search warrant, they roamed freely and finally confiscated a sizable quantity of electronic gear despite claims that it had nothing to do with phones. Then they marched him off to jail.

At the county jail, he found that he was one of five men arrested that night. One of the other four was his friend. He didn't recognize any of the others, but it didn't make any difference. The blue box had been found in the home of his friend.

Although the equipment taken from his home was in no way related to phone phreaking, it was put on display for newsmen to take pictures of, along with the five fraud conspirators. As the newsmen poked about, a Bell publicist told all who cared to listen that the company intended to crack down on phone phreaks and their strange little toys—the blue boxes. Then the five men were released.

The next day, he lost his job. Within the week, civil defense let him go. Wherever he went seeking work in his field, he went unhired. His reputation preceded him.

His phone would go dead for days at a time for no explainable reason. He noticed an additional wire running from his phone connection plate. A loyal friend told him that it ran to the local Phone Company office. The company refused to disconnect it.

The legal case pending against him fell through when his lawyer obtained a motion of denial because the evidence against him had been collected illegally. Bell immediately announced that it would file an appeal—although it hasn't done so yet and it's been three years since his arrest. Bell wasn't through, however.

Two nights after his court appearance, his house was broken into. Several pieces of electrical equipment were all that was taken.

One night a few weeks after that, a stranger appeared at his door asking him where he had gotten his blue box. When told that there never was a blue box, the stranger hit him hard enough to cause internal bleeding. It took two phone calls and three hours for the police to arrive.

On the day the charges against him were dropped, Bell officials called a news conference. Announcing a full-scale war against the phreaks, whom it termed "a great threat to national security," Bell expressed outrage that the charges had been dropped by the "over-lenient courts," and vowed to redouble its efforts to stop the spread of so serious a crime. It was nearly as good as its word. In 1972, 37 phone phreaks were apprehended. In 1973, the total rose to 62.

> The right of the people to be secure in their persons, houses, papers, and effects, against unreasonable searches and seizures, shall not be violated, and no warrants shall issue, but upon probable cause, supported by oath or affirmation, and particularly describing the place to be searched, and the persons or things to be seized.[1]

Coiners and Other Thieves

One of the easiest marks for criminals to hit are coin telephones. Seldom protected, easily accessible, and without alarms to prevent illegal access, coin telephones are knocked over with unbelievable frequency.[2] There is only one problem encountered in robbing coin phones: What do you do with all that change?

This small problem often enables the police to apprehend coin felons quickly. When three men strode into a Denver bank and asked to convert change into bills, the teller was not ready for the deluge of coins that followed. It took four hours to count the $6,000 in nickles, dimes, and quarters, but the men who brought it in didn't collect a single dollar bill. The bank, alerted to a recent string of phone robberies, called the law and announced that three men were in the bank with an extraordinary number of coins. The police arrived before the teller had counted out the first thousand and took the men into custody.

Most robberies are not conducted on such a scale, however. Usually, coin robberies are petty-cash operations. For the phones most often robbed are those in out-of-the-way places,

---

1. The Constitution of the United States, Article IV.

2. In some cases, protection is available. *The Grass Roots Quarterly* reported that Phone Company security agents watched one coin phone for six years awaiting the arrival of thieves; none appeared until two weeks after the detail was dismissed.

and phones in out-of-the-way places seldom draw much business. Also, the racket created in a robbery is bound to draw attention to the act. Even if the robber is armed with the special tools needed (bolt splitters, needle bars, etc.), unnatural activity can be noted by passers-by if the phone is in the open and, if it's in a booth, the working space is quite small. For these reasons, coin robbers generally take the phone with them if at all possible so that they can pry into it in relative privacy. Depending on local booth-construction practices, this can be hazardous:

One carload of Chicago coin thieves was apprehended as they drove down the street dragging a phone booth behind their car.

In an episode right out of the movie *American Graffiti,* two would-be thieves attached one end of a stout chain to a coin phone and the other end to their car. They sped off with the intention of taking the phone with them, but they had no idea how well the phone was anchored. Upon reaching the end of the chain, the drive shaft of their car parted company with the rest of the vehicle. The phone remained firmly in place. The men took off the car's license plates and walked away.

When determined robbers in New York found the phone bolted to the wall of a laundromat, they decided it would be easier to take out a section of the wall than to detach the phone itself.

In spite of the problems, taking the phone offers a much higher margin of success than trying to get the money out of a phone in place. At least in Detroit it does. After ecologists cleaned out a municipal pond, they found 168 coin phones amid the sodden debris. All of them had been rifled.

Coin-phone fraud is another, much easier, way of finding your fortune (or winding up in jail) than abusing the little steel box.

Poor cousins of the toll-fraud machines known as blue and mute boxes are the fuzz boxes. These devices duplicate the tones of money dropped down the coin chute as heard by the operator or electronic equipment. If the device is sophisticated enough, there is virtually no chance of being caught unless security personnel physically catch the perpetrator in the act. And since no records are kept on individual calls made from coin phones, both the caller and the party called are safe.

At some colleges, airports, and other places where coin phones line the walls, fraud phreaks have been known to place their call on one phone and deposit the required change in one adjoining it. The sound of coins tinkling down the chute is identical on all coin phones in the same area, and so the operator or electrical equipment was deceived into thinking that the money had been deposited in the phone being used. Once the operator allowed the call to go through, the fraud phreak depressed the coin-return button of the phone with the money, finished his call, and walked away. The only means by which the Company could circumvent such activities was to either shorten the receiver cords so that they couldn't reach the phones on either side, or to place the phones far enough apart to make such activity impossible.

It has become a game of sorts. The company develops a coin phone that cannot be "worked," as coin fraud is called, and then the phreaks try to find a way to overcome the obstacle. The company thought it had a fool-proof instrument in the mercury-drop coin phone.

A mercury-drop phone works on the same principle as a thermostat. The coins trip a lever filled with mercury and the mercury completes the connection. The fraud phreaks got around this by using slugs—an old favorite—or by physically tilting the phone one way or the other. A mercury-drop phone installed in one fraternity house was later found by repairmen to swing freely in a complete circle. The frats had removed all but one bolt located almost exactly at the phone's center of gravity.

Another, more sinister, activity of coin phone devotees does not involve the phone itself, but rather the trucks used to haul away the loot.

Collection trucks are extremely attractive targets. They carry large sums of money, are seldom protected, and are almost never defended. In fact, the company goes to great lengths to impress upon its collectors the folly of defending the truck if a robbery takes place. It is a sensible philosophy. Seven out of eight phone collection truck robbers are caught within 48 hours because of the aforementioned problem of getting rid of all that change. It makes no sense to risk one's life for something the company has plenty of and can always get more of. The reason robbers of coin collection trucks are ·so quickly caught should be obvious. If $6,000 worth of nickles, dimes, and quarters is a lot of change, then $60,000 worth is ten times as much of a problem. The company is not using trucks for collections because it's fashionable. Trucks are the only vehicle that can handle the weight of the money, let alone the volume.

Toll Fraud

Toll fraud cost the company more than 142 million dollars in lost revenue in 1974, and preliminary figures for 1975 showed that the total might rise by more than 20 million. Inflation notwithstanding, the major reasons for toll fraud's increasing popularity are: 1. If done correctly, the chance of being caught is almost nonexistent. 2. It takes only slightly more intelligence to perpetrate toll fraud than it does to place a call legally. 3. More telephone equipment than ever is automatic, thereby increasing the chances for error. 4. More people than ever are fed up with the company and see toll fraud as a means of doing something about the situation.

To keep from getting caught, those who have performed these acts have had to know something about the way long distance calls are handled. Far too many would-be toll-fraud phreaks failed to realize that, to remain out of jail, they had to protect the recipient of the call as well as themselves. If the party billed for the call challenged the call, the company then turned to the party called. If it was an isolated incident, the company might well have let it pass as a mismarked toll ticket or a computer error. All of this was based on the assumption that the party called was aware of what the caller had been up to. In many cases, it was standard procedure to inform the person called that the company was being ripped off. If the perpetrator didn't take advantage of his friends and their good will, he survived. If there were too many calls being questioned that terminated at his friends' numbers, the company billed them for the calls. In that case, the friends sometimes turned in the fraud phreaks.

Some phreaks kept themselves and their friends out of trouble by billing their calls to another number. This is known as third-number billing and it, too, had to be handled with care.

They first located a company or firm in their area that had a large long-distance bill every month. Interstate collection agencies, large national corporations, regional wholesalers, and the like constituted the best bets. When they were ready to make calls, they told the operator to bill the call to the number of the company they selected. They only used this ploy at night since the Phone Company sometimes checks with the firm being billed to see if such a call is on the level. And they didn't make the call from their home phone, either. Many areas of the country have TSPS computer operator stations whose equipment enables them to tell at a glance the number where the call is originating from. If the phreaks gave them a phony number, the company knew something was amiss almost immediately. When the phreaks were billing the call to another number, they didn't pull a number out of the air and they didn't make their calls from a number where they were likely to be found later.

Another way fraud phreaks made free calls was to call collect when it was already arranged for the call to be refused by the other party. Many truckers and other over-the-road people used this ploy to send any number of prearranged messages. The only fault with this method was that the caller was restricted to conveying a message that said only what it was previously arranged for it to say. Trying to change messages in the middle of the stream was almost impossible. When a change of plans was in the works, they would either have to talk—and subsequently pay for the call—or forget the whole thing. This method worked only a few times, by the way. The company maintains a group of employees who do nothing but check on such abuses. When they have reason to believe fraud is close at hand, they can be most unreasonable.

Phony credit cards have worked sometimes. Those individuals who knew the credit card code—it is changed annually—could bill any number of calls to a nonexistent credit number and get away with it as long as the company didn't catch on to the trick. Here again, they avoided capture by moving around. They changed the phony number frequently and never called the same number more than twice when using the same credit number.

By far the most successful way phreaks completed calls without paying for them was to use one of the celebrated boxes. If they were caught, however, they could expect the worst. The company hates the box phreaks as much as fire and brimstone preachers hate sin. If custom allowed, the company would have box phreaks drawn and quartered before sending them off to jail for life. This is not to say they are lenient with other toll frauds. You can go to jail for using any of the aforementioned ideas. Before you try any of these methods, remember, it is illegal to attempt to defraud the toll system. The whole scene can be a bad trip.

The Biggest Ripoff of Them All

Captured phone phreaks generally receive jail terms along the lines of one year for every $1,000 worth of service not paid for. Using this formula, we find that the Phone Company should be put away for the next 148,500 years. The reason? The Phone Company will receive an average of 16.5 million dollars annually over the next nine years without providing any services in return. No such prison term will be handed down, of course, but the matter should not pass unnoticed.

The groundwork for the scheme was laid during the early days of the Vietnam War. Needing a way to finance that sordid episode, the government came up with the idea of a 10 percent excise tax on telephone services. This was put into effect. While the telephone tax did not cover all of the war's expense, it brought in over 1.1 billion a year to help defray the cost. It also became the target of low-level war resistance.

People who refused to pay the tax as a protest ran into two problems: 1. When the amount withheld got too big, the com-

pany cut off their service. 2. The Internal Revenue Service
sometimes got into the act in a big way. The first difficulty
was not nearly as serious as the second. Although the IRS
acted in only a few instances, those few were memorable.

In California, where one man built up an unpaid balance of
fourteen dollars, the IRS confiscated his car. In another case
in Georgia, the taxmen attached the scoundrel's home for
sixty unpaid tax dollars. In these and other cases, the company suffered acute embarrassment because of IRS's somewhat heavy-handed actions. Despite the company's efforts to
keep such incidents at a minimum, they continued to come to
light occasionally throughout our involvement in the war.

As the war wound down, the revenue derived from the tax
shifted to other uses. The uproar of the anti-war activists
died down, but the demand for the end of the excise tax grew.

Acting to placate a nation angry over rising taxes, the government decided to eliminate the telephone tax—gradually.
The government announced that the excise tax rate would
drop by one percent annually beginning in 1973. At this point
the plot thickens.

During the heyday of the phone tax, phone users paid 10
percent on the monthly service. If the monthly service cost
$100, the tax due was $10. Beginning in 1973, the tax in all
fifty states should have been $9 on the hundred, but it wasn't.
It was $9.27 in some, $9.45 in others. In almost every state,
the tax was more than $9, and the government wasn't getting
the overage. The Phone Company was.

On the day the government lowered the tax rate to nine percent, the company began calculating the telephone tax on the
monthly service *plus* any state taxes that applied. On a
monthly billing of $100 with a state tax rate of 3 percent, the
excise tax due was still $9, but the company collected an ad-
ditional twenty-seven cents on the state's $3 tax. Twenty-
seven cents may not seem like much, but consider that the
company collected twenty-seven cents on every hundred dollars it took in. The total take that first year was 29.7 million
dollars.

This charge, which was approved by a federal court, will
decrease every year—in 1974, it was 26.4 million—until it fi-

nally disappears altogether in 1982, along with the excise tax. But by that time the company will have skimmed off $148,500,000. . . .

Company Hijinks

The company that screams foul whenever it is the target of low crimes and assorted misdemeanors has been known to commit some dubious acts of its own. The most widely recognized Telephone Company transgression lies in its ability to tap in anywhere at any time. Theoretically, the company has the right to do this since the line belongs to them—remember, customers only *lease* equipment. As any company publicist will tell you, any property owner wants to keep an eye on his holdings. It's a sign of level-headed and sound management. The truth of the matter isn't so lofty.

Often a phone employee will tap into a line just to hear what he can. In private circles, many will admit as much. Men and women who work in the central offices do this to alleviate boredom during the long hours they spend trapped in an electronic maelstrom. If and when they come across illegal doings, they immediately notify security and are rewarded for their "high level of responsibility." Security may then spend the next few weeks listening in, gathering information, trying to discover some means of *legally* catching the felons. It must do this since wiretapping is illegal and can result in an airtight case being thrown out of court if handled incorrectly. Security wants the subject to make some move that will put him squarely in the clutches of the law. It's usually fairly easy to accomplish since the evildoers don't realize they are being listened to.

On a lower plane, central office personnel can be the most knowledgeable people in town about local sexual activities. Probably no less than nine out of ten switchmen know where the neighborhood hotpants can be found from listening in on calls. When switchmen get together, they trade "hot numbers" with other switchmen in much the same way that children trade baseball cards.

Operators are also guilty of tapping in on calls, but much more infrequently and for different reasons. Usually operators will only listen in on calls they have helped place just to see what was so important. Operator taps are so infrequent when compared to the numerous switchmen taps as to be all but noncomparable.

The authorized taps—in this sense meaning taps that the company is aware of and ordered—take many guises. The latest ploy is a nationwide line check on all one-line and two-line customers to detect unauthorized line attachments. Although the company claims this can be done without violating customer privacy, few technicians take this claim without a grain of salt. If an unpaid-for piece of equipment is found on a line, then the company moves into another area where they can be contrary—that of customer service.

If a customer is found to have unauthorized equipment in his home or business, the company will first ask the customer to take the equipment out or start paying for it. If the customer fails to do as the company demands, the company simply cuts off the service. It does this for a wide selection of sins and the threat never fails to give the company leverage when dealing with the recalcitrant. If a customer has an unpaid bill, if he speaks harshly of the company, if he disregards company policy, or for any other reason that sounds plausible, a service rep may direct her central office cohorts to pull the plug. To add insult to injury, there is a reconnection charge to have the service restored. Essentially, the customer subsidizes his own punishment. If he refuses to pay this charge, the company will disconnect his service again.

It does no good to purchase equipment, either. Since the Telco owns the lines, failure to measure up to their lofty standards of equipment manufacture can mean suspension of service for as long as the company sees fit. If the company doesn't like the buyer's attitude, it can make owning equipment as difficult as using company-provided gear by cutting service off for days and possibly weeks at a time, while claiming line problems or central office overloads. The company will blame outside equipment, shoddy installations, the weather, practically anything but its own gear. In fact, it isn't even necessary to have outside equipment to be put through this gauntlet. The company blames interconnects for all types of service problems. If a customer is so bold as to actually have foreign gear, the company will make excuses whenever something goes wrong. By blaming outside equipment, the company makes its interconnection report look good in the eyes of the State Public Service Commission and causes problems for those who no longer choose to use company-provided service.

Those who remain in the fold have problems of their own, although they may not realize it.

That the company uses its position to its own advantage as much as it can has already been established. It plays both sides against the middle and the middle against both ends with great finesse. Business customers are pressured into leasing services they may not want by the company's pointing out that their competitors have that particular service. It may be that the competitor would have preferred to keep such information confidential, but it makes no difference to the Phone Company in its search for equipment sales.

The company can use its unique position to bid on equipment and services long before the competitive phone suppliers know that bids are being sought, since one of the first things planned in new offices is the phone wiring arrangements. The logical place for architects to find information is the Phone Company, and the engineers never fail to give the other departments the news. By the time potential competitors learn of construction, the company already has the contracts signed and the installation crew ready. An interconnect company salesman told me that one potential client declined his offer of a bid because "the Phone Company told me their bid would be the lowest." Such people deserve what they get.

The company also tends to leave its employees on too free a leash with confidential customer information.

Shortly after nonpublished numbers began costing a dollar a month, a service rep in the Northwest started supplementing her income by selling the silent-number lists to street-address directory firms and mailing-list companies.

One accounting clerk moonlighted by selling customer numbers to a collection agency.

A business office secretary added to her income by selling long distance usage sheets to a supplier of auxiliary office equipment.

A directory salesman received a healthy Christmas bonus from the company he supplied with confidential directory information.

A marketing rep bought a new car with the money he received from selling pre-planning information to a construction company.

The company seems almost indulgent in those cases where employee hanky-panky involves free enterprise. But Hell hath no fury like a company that finds *itself* being sold.

One individual began collecting information on the company's shortcomings. In an attempt to learn more, he brought others from other departments and areas into the picture. Together, these employees gathered a wealth of data on all facets of the company's activities. For three years they acted in concert, trading anecdotes and trying to verify everything they heard—even going to the extent of copying company memos. Then one of the women involved was caught seeking information on repair volumes and percentages. When her job was threatened if she failed to tell all, she told. The ringleader was brought before the high command and told to return and forget about every piece of information he had collected thus far. He refused, and three days later was fired for being a "recalcitrant employee." The company thought that would be the end of it. They were wrong.

Three sections of this book were already on paper. . . .

"Watergate Is a Gnat Compared to the Bell System"[1]

Sometime before eleven on the autumn morning of October 17, 1974, T. O. Gravitt shut the doors and windows of his suburban Dallas garage and started the engine of his car. Death,

---

1. This section is based partly on information obtained in interviews with James Ashley conducted in January of 1975. The author attempted to get the Bell System's side of the story on four consecutive days in that same month. He was refused access to anyone in an official capacity.

in Gravitt's estimation, was the only sanctuary from what he saw as systematic persecution aimed at him and the only solution for his sense of disillusion. Whatever else may have contributed to his wish to die, he felt that he had been hounded unmercifully by the company to which he had given more than twenty years of devoted service, and that he had had no opportunity to reply to scurrilous charges and outrageous implications, which, he stated in a suicide note, had caused "irreparable damage" to his reputation.

In death Gravitt achieved what he could not in life. He opened doors that had never been opened before. For the first time the general public was allowed inside the Bell System's high-level offices. For the first time the public could see just how the Bell System exploits those it is supposed to serve and how it treats those who serve it.

Only a year earlier, Gravitt's suicide would have been inconceivable to anyone familiar with him, and especially to Gravitt himself. He was one of the rising stars within the Bell System, so highly thought of by the steadily dwindling number of men above him that his name was inscribed on Bell's gilt-edged "promotion list." From rural telephone salesman in 1947, Gravitt had risen to the position of Texas Operations Chief for Southwestern Bell, a job that put him in charge of 38,000 employees, 6 million telephones, and 3.5 million dollars' worth of other equipment. Had he been willing to play by the rules of Texas telephone management, he undoubtedly would have attained even greater stature. He might still be alive, too.

Texas, unlike forty-nine other states, has no state utilities commission. The ruggedly individualistic state of Texas prefers to let its cities and municipalities handle their own utilities cases. The result of this rugged individualism is that ruggedly individualistic Texans pay higher utilities rates than anyone else in the nation. This being the case, it should come as no surprise to learn that Southwestern Bell, the Bell Company serving Texas, makes more money than any other Bell Company. And of the five states under Southwestern Bell's jurisdiction, the biggest revenue-producing state is— you guessed it—Texas.

Gravitt knew as much before he came to the state. In a 1972 memo, J. M. Good, vice-president and Southwestern Bell rate expert, wrote, "There is no question but what the Southwestern [Bell] approach in Texas rate cases is out of step with its approach in Missouri and Kansas and with that used by other Bell System companies." Welcome to Texas, Mr. Gravitt.

Good continued, "So far this may have resulted in more good than bad." Good informed Gravitt that rate cases in Texas might get touchy unless "present rate structuring" was amended, and he warned Gravitt that "Southwestern's present position might become extremely difficult to defend in court. It is my opinion that Southwestern would lose such tests." What Good was trying to tell Gravitt was that the gravy train was about to derail unless a strong hand was employed. To better illustrate what was going on in the state, Good prepared a graph showing the maximum rate increase each city in Texas would accept without starting an investigation. Beneath this chart, he included a graph showing the minimum rate increase Southwestern Bell was willing to accept for each of the listed cities. In every instance, Bell was receiving two percentage points more than what it actually needed to sustain a profitable operation. Gravitt's new job would be a delicate balancing act. He was sophisticated enough to realize that he was expected to out-produce his predecessor, but he also realized that he was walking into a hornet's nest of Texans fed up with Bell's exploitation. It would not be easy. Not for a man of Gravitt's character.

Gravitt was known as a fair-minded if tough man to work for. He expected maximum effort, but always within the confines of accepted business practices. We do not know what reservations Gravitt may have had regarding his new position. But from the record he left, we do know that he did his utmost to eliminate some of the more blatant practices commonly found in Texas.

For example, Bell expects every one of its operating divisions to show a rate of growth over 6%. During the mid-60s, the rate of growth in Texas was leap-frogging annually at a rate of 17%, which made everybody happy. But inflation was causing this growth rate to slip. In a frantic effort to maintain past growth trends, Bell management in Texas began sacrificing service to save profits. Service was actually getting as bad as New York's, but Bell management turned a blind eye. Gravitt arrived, saw what was happening, and moved to stop the deceptive growth patterns. He stepped on many toes by giving priority to service over profits throughout the state. What he did was commendable, of course, but people who had begun to believe their own lies were enraged.

Even so, Gravitt might have gotten away with his reform program if he hadn't made his superiors look bad. Some of the men who ran Texas before Gravitt's arrival had initiated the very practices Gravitt was trying to stop. These men, every one now higher on the chain than Gravitt, realized that if Gravitt was successful it would be a repudiation of everything they stood for—it would make them look bad. To ensure their own survival, Gravitt had to be stopped. The only question was how. Through one of Gravitt's staff, the high command saw a way.

James Ashley, an assistant vice-president, was responsible for handling rate cases throughout the state of Texas. When he had arrived on the job, he found that some of the rate experts on his staff were veterans familiar with every trick of the trade—some of which can only be described as appalling. Blackmail, bribery, and pork-barreling were sometimes used to get rate hikes.

It's to Ashley's credit that he believed these practices had no place in rate cases and that he moved to put a stop to them. He had come to Texas from Kansas at about the same time that Gravitt had. They had known each other, worked together, and, most important of all, trusted each other for years. When Gravitt took over, he put Ashley in charge of rate cases because he knew that Ashley would do the job properly. But neither of them was prepared for the morass they found.

Ashley wondered why one particular commissioner was so

fervently pro-Bell. When he saw the terms of the multimil-
lion-dollar contract awarded to this commissioner's firm,
he understood. He became familiar with Bell's double-stan-
dard approach in computing profit margins: the double depreciation of telephone poles, the "fair-value" appraisals of
buildings, and the double writeoff of bad debts through
Southwestern's books and those of A. T. & T. He saw the transcripts of wiretaps placed on commissioners' telephones,
and he saw how corporate high living was written off as
normal business expenses. He told all to Gravitt.

For their pains, according to Ashley, both men were
warned by S. W. B.'s General Manager to stop "all this
damned crusading" or there was going to be trouble. They did
not stop and there was trouble.

In late September, 1974, Texas was deluged with security
agents asking questions about Gravitt and Ashley. Their
questions were neither subtle nor discreet. If Gravitt's suicide note can be believed—and there has been no reason yet
put forth why it should not be—the main line of the question-
ing had to do with sex: "Have you gone to bed with him?" or
"Has he made a pass at you?" No one was asking about corporate malfeasance, just sex.

Gravitt became aware of the interrogations; he could not
help noticing that every member of his staff—over 150
people—was hauled into the spotlight by the security men.
He demanded to know the reason for the investigation and
was told that it did not concern him. Even for Bell this was
blatant, but Gravitt was helpless. The security agents did
everything but directly accuse Gravitt of hanky-panky, but
at the same time they refused to let Gravitt defend himself.
He was denied access to the interviews in which his name
was bandied about. He was told not to worry one instant and
threatened the next. Finally, in early October, security let
Gravitt in on the plot.

We want Ashley, he was told by the security people. Help
us get him and we will leave you alone. If this was the goal of
all that had transpired, then the reason Gravitt had not been

immediately informed of the investigation has been conveniently ignored by Bell in press conferences. But it should be obvious why Bell will not supply an answer. It can't.

In the first week of October, Ashley was suspended pending an investigation. He was questioned. According to Ashley, he was told that if he would give Bell "the goods on Gravitt" he would be reinstated. Ashley refused, and his suspension was formally changed to a termination. The reasons given were "certain irregularities in expense vouchers and business practices."

Gravitt's persecution continued. Repeatedly he was told that he was not under investigation, but the interrogations continued and Gravitt was not allowed to attend. He had to do something. On October 12, he and Ashley met to discuss the matter.

The two men decided to send a lawyer to headquarters in St. Louis to tell Bell to stop this irresponsible slander or to prepare for a legal fight. He was to further inform Bell that if it did not cease and desist, Gravitt and Ashley were prepared to expose political slush-funding, wiretapping, rate fixing, and corporate hijinks among some of the executive officers. In St. Louis the lawyer was told that if Gravitt wasn't happy he should talk things over with his superiors. He was assured that the investigation then in progress did not involve the already dismissed Ashley. At about the time the lawyer was leaving Bell's offices, Gravitt was starting his car. . . .

Up to this point, everything had been kept under wraps. But the little that had filtered through to the surface strongly suggested that a high-level executive was being investigated for irregularities. When the news of Gravitt's death was released, Bell publicly stated that the two were not related. Privately, though, Bell was telling favored reporters that not only were the two related, they were actually one and the same. When that news was made public, Bell's statement on the matter made it look as though Gravitt had killed himself rather than live in disgrace. Bell did not tell the press what it had told Gravitt. Bell denied that it had been playing each man against the other and cynically, it seemed to some, called for an end to such post-mortem harassment of Gravitt. Again, however, subsequent behind-the-scenes activity bore no relation to the public statements. Gravitt was dead and could no longer defend himself, so all Bell had to do to bring the matter to a tidy conclusion was to get Ashley to see things its way. It never occurred to Bell that friendship might preclude that. As Ashley tells it, here's what happened:

At Gravitt's funeral, Chet Todd of Southwestern Bell expressed great shock at having read in the San Antonio papers that Ashley might sue the Company. Todd told Ashley that he would be completely discredited if he attempted such a thing. Ashley, unable to believe that Bell would be callous enough to bargain at a funeral, declined to discuss the matter, but Todd persisted.

According to Ashley, Todd told him that if he would drop the matter, Bell was prepared to authorize $120,000 in severance pay and an annual pension of over $20,000 a year—a $400,000 package. Ashley replied that he could not come to terms with the company that had caused his friend's death. Todd, he said, swore at him and left.

The tactless actions of Bell's representative at Gravitt's funeral served to stiffen the resolve of Ashley and Gravitt's family. When Bell continued publicly to denounce both men, Ashley and the Gravitt family filed suit in state court. They asked for damages of 29.2 million dollars. They charged Bell with defamation of character, libel, and slander. Bell countered their charges with some of its own: sexual hijinks (both airborne and on the ground), misuse of company funds, and mismanagement. The Bell charges led to the most serious allegations of the tangled case. Ashley and Gravitt's family charged Bell with four further indiscretions, the ones the lawyer had presented to Bell on the 17th: political slush-funding, wiretapping, rate fixing, and executive hijinks.

This gave Bell immediate cause for concern, as evidenced by Ashley's final interview with the Bell Company. According to Ashley, the conversation went something like this:

Todd: What do you think would be a fair settle-
          ment?
Ashley: There is none. I have to go ahead with
          this.
Todd: Would this change your mind? [Todd then
          showed Ashley a press release com-
          pletely exonerating him of all charges.]
          All you have to do is forget about this
          lawsuit.
Ashley: That's not acceptable.
Todd: Would you give me your word to wait on
          this suit for two months before you file?
          I'm sure we could see fit to keep you on
          the payroll during that time.
Ashley: That is not acceptable.

This was the last of the one-on-one meetings. All subsequent collisions occurred in the courtroom, and will be a
matter of public record when a court-ordered "gag rule"
is lifted after the case actually goes to trial. At this
point, it would be wise to review the charges and countercharges. First, Bell's charges:

KICKBACKS ON RIGHT-OF-WAY LEASES: This charge is
one of the first Bell made public. One must ask what the Operations Chief for an entire state and his rate expert were doing
at meetings on such a low level. Right-of-way leasings entail
the placement of telephone poles and the digging of holes for
underground cables. If Ashley and Gravitt were indeed receiving kickbacks, they weren't getting much. Right-of-ways
fall under the category of eminent domain, involve no money,
and are negotiated with homeowners and other property
owners. In most areas, such negotiations are handled by a
first-level supervisor.

SEXUAL MISCONDUCT: Bell alleges that Gravitt tried to
manhandle a Business Office Supervisor in his airplane
10,000 feet up while the plane was on automatic pilot. Bell
also contends that Ashley and Gravitt forced female employees to have sex with them to keep their jobs. This author

contacted four women whom Bell implicated in the case. None of them mentioned blackmail, nor was force even discussed. The consensus among them was that it was none of Bell's business what happened after hours.

MISUSE OF COMPANY FUNDS: Bell contends that both Ashley and Gravitt falsified vouchers. This is the pot calling the kettle black. (See memo attached to Gravitt's suicide note.)

MISMANAGEMENT: Bell claims that Gravitt's poor leadership resulted in huge deficits in its San Antonio operation. If any loss accrued under Gravitt's direction, it is most probable that it was caused by Gravitt's refusal to doctor the books as his predecessors had done. People who knew Gravitt well contend that his first priority was service. Service costs money, and the people of San Antonio credit Gravitt with improving their service. If Gravitt and Ashley were poor managers, why did they carry the highest possible Bell personnel ratings, and why were they both on the promotion list?

The charges of Ashley and Gravitt are best described in Ashley's own words. When questioned about his allegations, Ashley had the following comments:

RATE FIXING: "Texas is the only state in the union that has no state regulation of utilities. Texas, in the past twenty years, has produced more money for the Bell System than any other state. Bell manages to do this by manipulating the fair-value system of depreciation and rate base, which enables it to show low net worth at tax time and a low net worth-to-investment ratio when petitioning for higher rates on services. It also aids its cause to handle rate increases on the municipal level. No municipal government has the capability of contesting the overwhelming legal and economic staff at Bell's disposal. Here, too, the tactic of infiltrating the local community by joining civic groups and utilizing local services helps immensely. Political campaign contributions made by executives to candidates favored by the company and other such low methods of control seal the city's fate."

SERVICE PROBLEMS: "Every man who assumes a new position in the company is expected to equal the growth performance of his predecessor if not surpass it. When inflation hit an area in the late 60s, the current managers had to make sacrifices to keep growth patterns in line with the past. The first thing sacrificed in an effort to keep up was long-term maintenance, then long-term service requirements. It was a case of milking the golden cow for too long."

WIRETAPPING: "Information was passed between myself and Gravitt, and between myself and subordinates, that no one could have known about if they had not been listening in on the call. I am aware of such things going on because it happened while I was in St. Louis."

CORPORATE HIGH LIVING: "There are many cases I could tell you about, such as using company jets for personal junkets to Las Vegas, Florida, and Palm Springs, but Gravitt's note says it better than I could."

POLITICAL SLUSH-FUNDING: "Bell has had, in the twenty-three years I was with the company, a political slush fund. From 1951, when I started with the company, until 1966, the slush fund worked like this: every month the vice-president called on the department heads and received from them a sum of money. The amount varied. One month it might be $50, but election time might raise that to $200 a man. The department head covered this expense by falsifying vouchers, either in his own name or in the name of subordinates. In 1966, the powers that be became afraid that an outside audit might reveal patterns in this false voucher system, so a new system was devised. In that year, a very high official of Southwestern Bell authorized $1,000 raises for all fifth-level-and-above managers. These men were told in no uncertain terms that the raise was given solely to meet political contribution requirements. Every month, a General Staff manager would act as the bagman, making his rounds collecting the approximate $50 from all area people. This system was used continuously until the campaign reform laws of

1974 went into effect. Once the law went into effect, it became illegal for companies to make political contributions, so Bell told its people to write personal checks to the candidates of Bell's choice. It often happened that the contributor never met or even heard of the recipient of his 'donation.' The Gravitt family has in their possession a memo to the late Mr. Gravitt, telling him to write checks to five candidates. The family also has the canceled checks filled out per the requirements of the Bell memo."

Bell has repeatedly denied that such contributions were ever made under its orders. But a new witness came forward in January of 1975 who gave credence to Ashley's claims.

John A. Ryan, former vice-president and general manager of Southern Bell's North Carolina operation, told wire service reporters of making political contributions in a manner identical to that described by Ashley. Southern Bell denied that such things were happening now, but refused to comment on Ryan's charges of what had transpired the year before.

The charges and countercharges currently being tossed around in Texas and North Carolina have caused many states to look into Bell shenanigans in their areas. Missouri has uncovered evidence of political junketeering courtesy of Bell, and Kansas investigated evidence of improprieties in dealings between Bell and its state regulatory commissioners. Before the investigations run their course, we may find that Gravitt was right: That Nixon's Watergate was only a gnat compared to Bell.

The following is the text of the Gravitt suicide note as given to this author by Ashley. It has been edited slightly for purposes of clarification. Some items have had to be omitted because of illegibility in the copy of the note supplied to Ashley.

10-17-74

Ever since last Thursday, I have not been able to keep my head from spinning. It hurts and I feel bad.

I am afraid of brain damage. My right arm has started to go to sleep.

This coupled with the fact that the Bell System has permitted some of our people to question over 150 people and in so doing has caused me irreparable damage to my reputation. Questions like:

1. Have you bought him gifts at his request?
2. Have you fixed him up with women?
3. Have you gone to bed with him?
4. Has he made a pass at you?

This is unfair for a Co. to do this without letting me be present.

They have accused me of being partial with contracts. This is totally untrue.

I did try to get reimbursed for using my airplane. It was used for company business and to haul politicians.

They have accused me of having financial arrangements with Quik Print. This is totally untrue. I have known Bill Gravely for 10 years. We have been in each other's homes.

I worked through Western Electric and Marvin Reed in trying to get a better traffic record job in Texas. Bill Gravely turned out to be the best qualified and cheapest. He never gave my Co.[1] one cent, only quality work.

I think records should be subpoenaed according to attached memo.

Also is memo showing a few things others have done.

There is bound to be much more. Watergate is a gnat compared to the Bell System.

---

1. Southwestern Bell.

T. O. Gravitt

Have Mike see a good lawyer. . . .

Company paying personal expense

> Following Hemisfair, what happened to golf carts, furniture, & other valuables.

> Co. Lease—_____ did work on roads, blinds, house, trailer house, & charged work to other projects. What happened to vehicles, furniture, guns, trailer house & other improvements.

> _____ bought many pictures for _____ & charged to Company.

> _____ insisted & has concurred in hunting arrangements for 4 days. Cost about $500. Has done every year.

> _____—White wine hunting cost $900. 2 days.

> Our people pay hotel bills for all exec. _____, _____, _____, _____.

> _____ told me of spending over $1500 to fix leaking basement in _____ home. . . .

Trips

> _____ and _____ to Mtn [Mountain] Bell about 6-25-74 (Fri) to talk about El Paso settlements. Took wives & stayed all weekend.

> _____ to Dallas all week for

Byron Nelson Open. Spent 1 hour in office (with wife).

_____ to Waco a few years ago. Party for 200 people cost $2000. Before this on Monday, jet to Lubbock (deadhead back to St. Louis). Wednesday picked up in Lubbock to McAllen after stopping in San Antonio for _____ (jet deadhead to St. Louis) Thursday charter to Waco, Friday jet picked up in Waco.

_____ jet to see daughter several times. Once to move her personal belongings, 6-1-74.

_____—jet with wife to see daughter in play. _____ entertained.

_____—jet to Wichita with family for wedding also to Topeka for board meetings.

_____ to Columbia attend football game & voucher expense. 10 times to Bracketville, 2 times McAllen, 2 times to Dallas, 1 from Hot Springs.

_____ _____ & _____ _____ used their plane. No approval.

_____ to Houston to attend bank meeting.

Jet charter to pick up _____ returning from personal vacation.

_____ taking jet to Oklahoma City from St. Louis then to San Antonio (personal).

Jet trips to Florida for other corp. officers.

_____   chartered   plane   for
_____, TOG[1] & _____ who
signed correct.

Guerrilla Action on the Phone Front

In the legion of those who distrust and hate the Phone Company are a few "dedicated" men and women who have pur-
posefully attacked the giant wherever and whenever they
could, and this book would not be complete without some
mention of them as societal renegades who have fought back
and often paid the price for doing so. I don't condone their
actions and I'm not advocating the widespread use of terror
tactics—even if you feel oppressed, swindled, or just impo-
tent in the face of this enormous cartel—because the punishment can be worse than the crime you are protesting. But
here, in the interests of reporting the facts about social unrest
in Telephone Land, are a few of the methods the radicals have
used to strike back:

One of the most damaging—and most illegal—stratagems
is the ever-growing field of toll fraud. Some methods people
have used to accomplish this feat are so complex that only an
M. I. T. grad could hope to achieve solid success with them.
Some are still so widespread—and therefore socially
significant—that they have already been covered in greater
detail. But let me make it clear once more that *you can go to
jail for toll fraud* and that the odds are on the side of the Phone
Company no matter how original and foolproof you think
your system might be.

Those radicals with no desire to rot in a cell have found
other ways to come out fighting. A few individuals, feeling
that their bill was unjust, have cut additional holes in the
card that came with their bill. The result has been either a
load of laughs or a barrel of tears. One person who sliced up

---

1. T. O. Gravitt. The names of other company employees mentioned in the suicide
note have been omitted to spare them embarrassment, but all were, at the time, at the
managerial level or above—in at least one case, far above.

the punch card accompanying his April 1971 bill hasn't had a bill since. On the other hand, a young woman who tried the same trick with her December bill got a huge surprise in January when, instead of having to pay for her one cheap black telephone, she was billed for 387 red ones.

Another method that has had great popularity, without all of the uncertainty of hole-making, is the practice of controlled procrastination. Complicated, and requiring a high degree of patience and nerve, it has worked wonders, according to its devotees. All they do is withhold payment on their current bill until one day after the close of the next billing period (the date shown on the statement). When they receive the next bill, they pay only the amount shown as the *previous* balance (the amount unpaid from the last bill)—but they don't do so until the close of the next billing cycle. These radicals believe that if they keep this up for six months the company's accounting office will never get the mess straightened out. To prove their innocence of any wrongdoing, they keep check stubs of all payments made.

In the same vein, some radicals decided that they would be a little generous when their next bill arrived. They paid in excess of the amount due. The following month, they didn't pay quite enough to cover the charges. When the third bill arrived, they paid nothing at all until after the close of the next billing cycle. Such inconsistency, they reasoned, would keep the computers from tracking their payment record accurately. Here again, check stubs proved invaluable when the company called demanding an explanation of why the radicals were doing mean things to their computerized madhouse.

The college underground is still greatly in favor of placing long distance information calls to such places as Nome and Honolulu. Their argument is that these calls are free to the calling party and that they tie up long distance circuits, long distance operators, and lower the company's rate of return.

Some vindictive guerrillas have been known to order large quantities of phone equipment and then cancel the order at the last minute.

More extravagant guerrillas pay for each item shown on

their bill with separate checks, which they mail on successive days.

Playing by the Rules

If what society thinks of as the irresponsible approach doesn't appeal to you, there are legal methods that can be pursued peaceably. Every state in the union has some sort of regulatory body that governs Telephone Companies in the state. (Listings by state are in Appendix II.) If you feel that the company is unfair, unreasonable, or downright sickening, fire off a letter to your state's Public Service Commission explaining your gripe as objectively as you can. I have found that nothing puts the fear of God into a Telephone Company as fast as the threat of an executive complaint to the "Commission." If your complaint is in regard to interstate services, write to the Federal Communications Commission, 1919 M St., Washington, D. C. 20554.

Coordinated community action can do more good than many people usually believe. If the service in your area is intolerable, have petitions signed, hold public meetings, and by all means, get publicity. Bad publicity is feared by the Phone Company at all times but especially during rate hearings. In Blue Springs, Missouri, concerted community action resulted in the total re-engineering of the community's phone service. If your community cares enough about good service to do something about it, improvements will be achieved long before they might otherwise. But you must act.

Immediate Action

One night a few years back, a Phone Company vice-president attempted to place a long distance person-to-person call from his home and found out just how frustrating dealing with his company can be.

"This is the operator. Anything I can help you with?" Her voice was raspy. Apparently she was having a bad night.

The vice-president and general manager gave her all the necessary information she needed to complete his call.

"Could you give all that to me again, a little bit slower this time?"

So he did, but the exasperation was plainly evident in his voice.

"Did you know that you can dial this call yourself?"

He replied that he did, but that he wanted her to do it for him.

"Anything you say. But you'd save a lot of money if you dialed it yourself."

He repeated that he wanted her to dial it for him.

"Some people never learn." She probably didn't mean for him to hear her last remark, but he did and demanded to know her name. He threatened to have her head on a tray. Finally he even told her whom she was speaking to. And, once again, he demanded that she give her name to him.

"Wouldn't you like to know." With that, the line went dead.

It's comforting to know that other people—even Phone Company executives—catch hell every now and then just as we do. And this illustration illuminates one of the evils of the telephone that obscene callers have known about for years— the total anonymity of it all. If an operator or a service rep or a plant man feels like it, he or she can roast you verbally and there's very little you can do about it. True enough, such blatant discourtesy is rare but it does happen, and there are ways you can retaliate and get satisfaction.

If an operator is not everything you think she should be, immediately ask to speak with her S. A. A service assistant is a nonmanagement person who mediates disputes between operators in her group, helps with dialing problems, and distributes the "mark sense" tickets, the computer cards operators use to keep a record of each long distance call they handle. The S. A. has no real authority, but she takes a lot of the load off the person who does, the group chief operator. To an operator, the group chief is a mother figure, ally, and symbol of the all-powerful company all rolled into one. The group chief has the power of life and death in her kingdom, and a demand for an audience with her from an unhappy customer brings an unruly operator's heart to her throat. You may not get the privilege of actually talking to a group chief—that's what the S. A. is for—but the mere knowledge that you know that there is such an animal can straighten out the most obdurate operator.

Service reps generally don't give the customers a hard time for two very good reasons. 1. They have to give you their name before the conversation begins, and 2. the call itself often is bugged. Three hundred and sixty-four days of the year, you will seldom hear a disrespectful word from your service rep. But on December 24, the service observers go home early—it's generally the slowest day of the year—and no holds are barred. If you give the service rep a hard time, she's got a whole year's worth of frustration to take out on you. If you happen to get a harpy, demand to speak to her B. O. S. The Business Office Supervisor will generally stand behind her "girls," but in unusual cases she can and will have the offending service rep tarred and feathered.

The men you most often see are the linemen, the gallant knights of the Phone Kingdom. And there's a very good reason for their nobility: they're right there where you can hit them if they give you trouble. Usually the only time a lineman will give you a hard time is right after your dog has mangled his leg. If you should have a problem with him, the installation foreman is the man to talk to. The installation foreman is to the lineman what a group chief and a B. O. S. are to their respective sects. (Note: If you have reason to suspect that this person may not be from the Phone Company, ask to see his I. D. Card. It has his picture on it, his signature and the company logo.)

In summary, it's not what you threaten to do, it's whom you threaten to talk to that gives you an edge. The Phone Company has a jargon all its own, and the use of it by a mere mortal suggests that you know the ropes.

By the same token, there are times when the phone people really put it together and do an outstanding job. At times like that, it never hurts to put in a good word for the excellent service rendered. The word will get around, and you'll be surprised how well you'll be taken care of in the future.

Section IV: BUSINESS SERVICES

Only thirty-two percent of the Telephone Company's customers are business concerns yet businesses provide fifty-five percent of the Telephone Company's revenue. Using a formula no other utility company would dare implement, the Phone Company charges its large-volume customers more for each piece of equipment than it does its limited users. Only in rare instances do business customers receive price advantages and then only when such transactions would be in the Phone Company's best interest. Nor does the company offer gross-lot discounts on service. When it does, it invariably draws complaints from competitors and those unable to benefit from the discount.

Business customers have an unbelievably wide selection of higher-priced items to choose from. Ranging from simple one-line-one-telephone systems to complex nationwide operations, the business customer has a seemingly endless array of equipment and services to draw from that will handle his every need. If the equipment is not available, the company will redesign existing equipment to fulfill the demand.

Because of the many options available, and because the business customer has such a wide range to choose from, he can save time and money by reading what follows before instituting any changes in his telephone system. For, as we shall see, the Telephone Company is not the only source he can turn to for his phone service needs. . . .

Equipment

The simplest type of system available to the business customer is the single-line telephone like those in most homes. In most areas, the monthly charge for the phone is included in the line rate and is therefore relatively inexpensive. If needs are simple there is no better offering available. Any number of these phone instruments can be placed in offices where each individual needs only one line. But the limitations of a single-line phone are painfully obvious to anyone who has ever worked with one. It has no hold button and once the line is busy, the phone is completely tied up for the duration of the call. (Note: There is a two-line phone. Identical to the single-line unit except for a small turnkey in the lower left-hand corner, it works like two single-line phones. If one line is in use, the other will not work. Why anyone should want one such phone is unknown.[1]) Unless price is your only consider-

1. Of course if there are two two-line phones, each with its own number, both lines are operative; then the turnkey works as a hold button to handle incoming calls.

ation, six-button phones work better and have more flexibility when the hold feature is desired and two or more lines are required.

When you have six or more buttons on your phones, you have what is known in the Phone Company as a key system. Key systems come in many shapes and sizes and are used by more business customers than any other system because they are flexible and dependable. The rate for lines associated with key systems is generally lower than that for trunks associated with a PBX[1] because intercom traffic can be routed by station users; the system is expandable from five lines to twenty-nine (one button on every phone is used for holding); and having one central answering point for all calls is simply a matter of choosing which phone you want to ring. The equipment needed to operate a key system occupies less space than a chest-high filing cabinet, and the addition or removal of equipment does not require months of planning and physical labor, which often upsets office routine. More important, subscribers are not required to keep any equipment longer than one month.

Theoretically, although a key system has unlimited growth potential, the most efficient and economical key systems have less than twenty lines and forty phones. Beyond that point a small PBX will better serve the customer's needs. If the key system becomes inadequate, compare the current key-phone expense to the cost of a PBX. If the additional cost of the proposed PBX is within fifty percent of what is now paid out for phone service, then consideration should be given to the PBX system. A PBX offers greater flexibility, more room for growth, and more features for the money. However, bear in mind that you should never lease more telephone equipment than is actually needed. If telephone needs are more or less static and are expected to remain so, if the cost of the proposed PBX would increase the monthly telephone bill by fifty percent or more, or if the addition of new features will not be

---

1. Private Branch Exchange—a switchboard- or console-controlled telephone system.

of any great benefit, upgrading should not be undertaken until one of these three conditions is met. Before installing a PBX, examine what is involved.

PBX service provides customers with many features not available to the key system customer. Central answering, screening of calls, placing of calls, heavy intercom traffic, constant trunk use, conferencing, and call transfers are all easily handled with PBX equipment. Since a PBX is operated much like the company's central offices, careful planning is needed before such a system is put into operation.

One of the more important points to remember when considering PBX systems is that failure to keep them for a predetermined period of time will result in your paying penalty charges. The company has a sizable sum of money tied up in its PBX systems and, to cover the investment, it requires that the customer sign a Termination Agreement. By signing a "T. A." the subscriber agrees to keep the PBX system for a set length of time—anywhere from one to fifteen years—and to pay a prorated amount (based on the type of system) if the system is removed prior to the expiration date. For example, a T. A. running for three years with an initial penalty figure of $13,500 means that for every month the system is kept, the T. A. will decrease by 1/36. At the end of thirty-six months, if the system is removed the subscriber owes nothing. But if at any time during the life of the T. A. the customer decides to move or remove the system, he owes the Phone Company the current fractional part of the whole. Since the Phone Company recognizes no excuse for disconnection as legitimate other than a proverbial Act of God, the customer is, for all intents and purposes, stuck with what he has, at least until the T. A. expires.

The length of Termination Agreements varies, depending on the type of system installed. If the organization is unwilling or unable to sign a long-term agreement and a PBX would definitely be beneficial, it would be better off leasing what is known as a "feature-by-feature" system in which each item installed is paid for separately. Trunks (lines), consoles or switchboards, phones, lights, special arrangements, and the

unseen equipment needed to make the system work are itemized on the total bill. Feature systems run from ten-line forty-
station units to gigantic phone arrangements with 250 lines
and 2,000 or more stations. Because everything is billed separately, the chance of being misbilled is magnified, but, in
consolation, the T. A. is of short duration. With hundreds of
pieces of phone equipment in your office, a phone removed
may go unnoticed by the Phone Company accounting department for years while the customer continues to pay for it.
(Some informed sources claim that as many as 90 percent of
all feature-system accounts are misbilled. I have seen adjustment vouchers filed by the Phone Company where customers
were overbilled for as long as four and a half years, but this is
the exception rather than the rule.) To avoid mistakes and
overbilling, have the Telephone Company run an inventory
of the equipment at least every two years—every year when
twenty or more changes are made, and every three months
when the phone arrangement is constantly being changed.

Should a time come when phone requirements change and
something more than a feature system is needed, the next
step is the ultimate: package systems, or their more sophisticated relative, Centrex.

The package PBX system is a paradox. It is more intricate
in operation than a feature system, but the billing is less complicated. With a package system, you have more standard
features available. The station user can transfer calls, put
calls on hold, arrange conferences, and add other parties
simply by depressing a switch hook—no buttons needed.
Trunks, operator positions, lights, intercom lines, and equipment are included in a flat monthly rate based on the number
of stations in operation. Should more equipment be needed
with no increase in the number of telephone stations, there is
no charge for the additions. In concept, it's beautiful. In actual practice, it can trap the unwary.

All those wonderful things that can be done from the station user's phone only work with incoming calls. To put outgoing calls on hold you need a six-button set and its accompanying monthly charge. To place a conference call, the

operator must set it up for you just as she does on feature systems. If the station user wants to add someone else to a call he placed, forget it. If more trunks are needed to handle the call load, it can take as long as sixteen weeks to get them. If it becomes necessary to drop below the minimum number of stations, either the system can be disconnected, with the payoff of the Termination Agreement soon to follow, or the customer may continue paying for the minimum number of stations even though there are no longer that many. On most package systems the T. A. runs from three to five years, so the customer had better hope that he doesn't have to move to another location or cut back during that time.

These problems arise with package systems mainly because the people leasing them don't fully understand what they are getting into. When people sit down with the company representative to discuss the possible ramifications of a PBX, they should be sure that they receive satisfactory answers to all of their questions. As the company rep describes the proposed system, a detailed explanation of how each particular feature pertains to the operation should be demanded. Only when everyone is satisfied should the rep be given the go-ahead. During installation, staying reliably informed of everything that's happening is paramount. Installers are notorious for being misinformed and can start a real panic if their word is taken for granted. Keep in touch with the one individual who knows what the overall picture is—the sales representative. Be sure to allow enough time to get the job done. With package systems, sixteen weeks is the average installation interval and twenty-six weeks is not unusual. If a company calls today wanting a package system in a month, one of three things will happen: 1. The customer ends up with a feature system. 2. The customer pays extravagant overtime charges. Or 3. The resultant mess is twice as bad as not having anything at all. If care is taken and every step is thought out logically, the cutover should be painless and smooth. It isn't most of the time.

[At the time of this writing, there are strong indications that the package PBX is about to join the magneto phone in

Telephone Limbo. Due to a recent restraint-of-trade suit filed in Texas, the Bell System is considering "unbundling," or offering package systems feature-by-feature. Officially this move will be taken to "offer the customer what they need and only what they want." For the record, the restraint suit—filed by competitors—contends that by offering unlimited trunking and features the Bell System is playing with loaded dice. Apparently the Bell System thinks so, too, or it would not be unbundling. The package concept is too lucrative to get rid of voluntarily, official reasons to the contrary.)

Centrex . . . the most advanced telephone system in use today. Not for every customer, but one that allows greater latitude than any other type of system. If a large organization—such as a hospital, a local government operation, a college, or a corporate headquarters—needs superb communications, Centrex will give it everything it needs and wants. Indeed, a Centrex system is so large that each one is assigned its own three-digit prefix and no single phone person can make the decision whether or not to put one in service. The Phone Company has a standing group of employees who decide whether or not you can have a Centrex. What is so grand about a Centrex that all this must be done? What is it that makes all the planning necessary?

Centrex automatically itemizes every station user's long distance calls, and outside callers are able to dial each station user directly without going through the switchboard. Other than that, Centrex is no different from a large package PBX. Because no two Centrex systems are exactly alike on the inside, because of the long hours of planning and order execution, and because so few organizations will ever have need of one, nothing more need be said about them other than this: One of the more formidable companies in the open-phone market field is United Business Communications, a subsidiary of United Telecommunications, better known as United Telephone Company. While U. B. C. makes its sales pitch in Bell System territories, the parent company quietly makes and receives all of its home office calls on a Bell System Centrex. . . .

Long Distance Services

If all of the wire and cable used by the Phone Company were spliced into a single strand, it would reach from the Earth to the Sun and back again three times, with many million miles left over. And much of that 641 million miles of wire is used in some way for long distance calling. In 1974, the latest year for which figures are available, the Phone Company handled more than 31 million long distance calls *a day*, and the figure is rising eleven percent every year. Can the network continue to handle the call load at acceptable levels? Yes, with a few exceptions. Mother's Day places an unbelievable load on the long distance network—it's the busiest day of the year—and, in times of national crisis, the whole network can render itself "inoperative." (Within minutes after President Kennedy's assassination, every toll center east of the Mississippi had busied itself out. Not until that night was some semblance of order reestablished.) But the Phone Company has taken great pains to keep the calls going through. A. T. & T. Long Lines, which maintains overall control of the long distance network, long ago set up an intricate organization to route calls from one city to another. Exactly how it works on a day-to-day basis is not public knowledge, but generally the system works like this:

A call originating in Phoenix first goes to the local central office serving the caller's exchange, where it is identified as a long distance call. An appropriate circuit is opened that takes it to the toll center serving all of Phoenix's central offices. From the toll center, it is routed to the nearest primary center that handles calls from several toll centers throughout Arizona. Assuming that all of the primary-level circuits are busy, the call will be sent to the nearest sectional center where toll calls from several state primary centers are handled. If all lateral circuits are busy here, the call is relayed to one of the seven regional centers strategically located throughout the country. This is the apex of the call's journey. From the regional center handling Phoenix long distance calls, the call is sent to the regional center closest to the point of destination. It then travels back through sectional center, primary center, and toll center, finally reaching the central office of the destination number where it is routed to the phone itself. The total elapsed time of the call completion interval is in the vicinity of ten seconds. At any level on the call's route, it may jump laterally to an identical-type center should the call load dictate, thereby shortening the completion interval. And the call may not take the shortest route between points, either. A call from Boston to Miami may go through the regional center in St. Louis if call loads on the eastern seaboard are critically heavy. Compared to the intricate detailed planning that went into the nation's long distance system, Operation Overlord was akin to a children's picnic.

Standard long distance calls come in three basic packages: direct-dial, station-to-station, and person-to-person, with rates structured to heavily influence your choice. Millions of dollars are spent to promote direct dialing, officially because it saves the caller so much money. The real reason is more pragmatic—the profit margin on a direct-dialed call is greater than the margin on a person-to-person call in spite of the higher charge for the latter. Direct-dialed calls have a profit margin of more than ninety percent because no equipment is involved except for what was already there anyway. The circuit is in place, the maintenance is negligible, and the service provided is completely do-it-yourself. Person-to-person calls, on the other hand, have to go through an operator (who costs money) and she lowers the rate of return. That's why, on person-to-person calls, the profit margin is only forty-five percent. Recently, the Phone Company introduced "Zero-Plus Dialing," which confuses the caller and raises the profit margin on operator-handled calls. The method of operation is exactly like that of One-Plus Dialing except for the first digit. After you dial, an operator asks you how you want to charge the call. You do most of the talking, all of the dialing, and still pay for the call as if the operator did everything.

The computation of long distance call rates is similar to the mystifying rate structuring employed by the airlines. You pay the day rate between 8 A.M. and 5 P.M. Monday through

Friday—it's the highest because that's when most long distance calls are made. From 5 P.M. to 11 P.M. Sundays through Fridays there is the evening rate: it's slightly lower than the day rate, but still fairly high because many resident customers place long distance calls during this time span. Between 11 P.M. and 8 A.M., the night rate is in effect. Finally, from 8 A.M. to 11 P.M. on Saturday and from 8 A.M. to 5 P.M. on Sunday, there is the weekend rate—the lowest of all. If the call is dialed direct, it is charged on a minute-by-minute basis instead of a three-minute minimum. The rate per minute is no different, but if very short calls are made the minute rate can work to your advantage.

Now if anyone thinks he has all of this clearly in mind, he should try to remember this special clause, quoted directly from a Bell Systems Rate Guide applying to holidays: "On Christmas Day, New Year's Day, July 4th, Thanksgiving Day, and Labor Day, evening rates apply except on weekends and after 11 P.M. when lower rates apply." To further complicate matters, time periods do not apply on station-to-station, person-to-person, collect, or credit-card calls, or to any other operator-assisted call, regardless of holidays.

When doing regular long distance calling, all Phone Company customers pay uniform rates based on mileage (see Appendix IV), but business customers can take advantage of several types of service with lower rates—if they have sufficient volume. The most widely used offering is WATS, or Wide Area Telephone Service.

WATS lines are not the budget-slicers that so many people think they are. They are in no way distinguishable from any other type of telephone line. They require no special equipment and, except in rare cases, little prolonged capital outlay. They are simply a direct-access line to the long distance network. For a set monthly charge, the user can make all the calls he wishes to a predetermined slice of the country. WATS is available in all 48 contiguous states but does not give the user access to Alaska, Hawaii, or any foreign country. The smallest interstate service area includes all the states bordering the user's own, and the largest area gives the subscriber access to all states in the continental U. S. excluding his own. (Home-state coverage—known as area 7 WATS—is available in every state, but it is a line by itself. No state offers inter-state and intrastate WATS in a single package.) The WATS areas—known as bands—are inclusive. If you have area 5 WATS, you also have access to areas 1 through 4. The company advertises WATS as the greatest blue-eyed bargain ever to slide down the pike, but when the limitations are ex-plained to potential customers the glamour diminishes some-what. If WATS lines were as economical as the company claims, there would surely be more than 105,000 in service.

What most discourages people from becoming WATS fans is the cost. The minimum monthly price is $135, the highest, $1,700. And just having $1,000 worth of long distance calls each month does not necessarily mean that WATS is going to work as planned. Since WATS only works one way—either incoming or outgoing—a wide diversification of calls can knock the potential customer out of the WATS ball game. The Phone Company uses a simple, easy-to-fudge-on formula called a toll study to determine whether a customer can use WATS. Because the WATS areas are fixed, they cannot be broken up to suit customer needs. Even if only a fractional part of a given area is all that is needed, the customer must lease access to the whole area. Because WATS rates are set, it is a simple matter of comparing regular long distance costs in a given area to the cost of WATS in that area. But time is im-portant, too. Exactly why involves a short detour from the present discussion.

WATS is available in two standard types, measured and full-business-day service. With measured service, an initial monthly charge for ten hours (in some places fifteen) that varies from $135 to $290 is charged, depending on which area is needed and which state you're in. Once the initial ten or fifteen hours is used up, the customer is not cut off—or even notified; the company simply bills him for the additional time used in tenths of hours. This additional hourly rate is lower than the first-period hourly rate by as much as twenty per-cent. The thinking behind this is that the more WATS time is used, the more money is saved over using the same amount of time on long distance. The trouble with this reasoning is that customers receive a nasty shock—as many WATS users have—when they get their bill for three or four thousand dollars.

If the long distance expense is extremely large, use full-business-day WATS. The rates run from $510 to $1,700. The phone can be left off the hook for 240 hours on the same call and the rate on this type of WATS service will not fluctuate. But only one WATS customer in ten is in a position to use full-business-day WATS because of its high monthly cost.

Time is money on WATS, and your people should be informed of this fact when you lease a WATS line. Many ten-hour measured-rate WATS customers have all but gone broke because someone in accounting has been talking to his sister for hours on the measured-rate WATS, thinking WATS means unlimited calling for a set price—which it doesn't.

This is why the amount of *time* spent on WATS long distance calls is just as important as the amount of *money* when a toll study is being run. If a company is spending an average of twenty-six cents a minute on regular long distance calls in WATS area 1, and area 1 WATS is thirty cents per minute, it's obvious that WATS is going to cost $30 more over a ten-hour period than is now being spent. By taking the amount of money already spent talking in a given WATS area and dividing it by the number of minutes used, the customer can see how much his long distance calls cost per minute. By comparing that figure to the cost per minute on WATS, he can tell whether WATS is the expected panacea to his high long distance expenses. If many long distance calls are being made from an office (out-of-office calls do not count), and they are less than five minutes long, then outgoing WATS may well be advantageous. If many calls come into an office now, or if a projected phone campaign is going to generate many calls coming into the office, then incoming WATS may be the answer.

The biggest disadvantages to WATS are: 1. that the customer has no idea how much time has been used on the line in any one month until the bill comes the middle of the following month and 2. usually no record of calls is provided at all. WATS is offered with the understanding that no monthly printout of calls will be made unless the customer wants to pay for it. In fact, that's the initial advantage of WATS from the company's standpoint, and why they can offer a discount. But while there is no computer expense, no key-punch expense, and so on, the absence of printed records can make for some nasty fights. If and when the company misbills a WATS-line customer—and, says one high-placed Long Lines source, about fifteen percent of all WATS bills are in error—there are no complaints about billing mistakes because the customer has no standard to guide him. But if the customer can provide any proof at all he did not use as much time as the company says he did, the company will generally back down. If the proof is not there—or if the company's monthly adjustment budget is depleted—then it's pay up or lose the service. Proof, luckily, consists of anything that sounds logical: sales records, operator logs, business volume charts, or a meter. WATS meters are offered by the company, but since the meters are tied into their equipment the chances that the meter in the customer's office and the meter in their office will disagree are, to be charitable, very slight. Several independent companies manufacture WATS meters. Most equal the Phone Company as far as service is concerned and beat it in price. Such equipment is fully independent of Phone Company gear, although both types work in an identical fashion. Some meters do not even need to be tied into the phone system.

Another of WATS' shortcomings is that, without firm control, it can cost more and give less coverage than using long distance exclusively. For example, with nationwide WATS coverage, you would think that no matter where the call goes WATS would be cheaper than long distance. But this isn't always so. All WATS rates are based on the area farthest away from the calling point to the forty-eight states in area 5. If you call an intermediate state in area 1 the call is paid for at band 5 prices, a difference of about twenty cents per minute used. If there is a need to place calls to points all across the country, ideally a customer should have five WATS lines, with their accompanying cost as well, but to save a dollar he may end up paying several hundred. Hence, the problem.

And what if the Phone Company's toll study indicates that to save money, only one WATS line should be used, and you have fifteen or twenty employees-who will have to use the same WATS line at the same time? This can wreak havoc with work schedules.

Another common control problem is free-for-all use. If the WATS line is easily accessible to everyone, eventually someone is going to start using it to call his sister on the opposite coast. And even if this doesn't happen, chances are the authorized users will one day discover that using the WATS is much easier and faster than writing interoffice memos. Customers must be able to control the use of their WATS line if it is to save them money.

The Phone Company likes WATS for a number of reasons, one it likes the most being that WATS users tend to use more long distance than non-WATS users. Even if the line is leased with the express purpose of reducing long distance expense, the Phone Company projects that within six months the total long distance bill will rise by about fifty percent. The company has long known that WATS users tend to forget rather quickly why they leased the line and start doing things on the phone that they never would have dreamed of doing before the WATS line came into the picture. WATS is a corporate toy that needs careful supervision. If you have one, hold a critical review of its value every six months or so. If telephone expense is rising faster than the company's growth would indicate that it should, dump the WATS line.

There are a number of restrictions on WATS that potential customers should be aware of. First and foremost, it is strictly against the law to refuse collect calls so that the WATS subscriber can call back on his WATS line. The Phone Phactory has a special investigative unit on the lookout for just this sort of thing. If it catches the malefactor in the act, he gets one warning before it pulls the coils.

It is also illegal to sublease a WATS line. The company

frowns on those entrepreneurs who try to rent out their equipment along with the office space. This, too, is an offense punishable by disconnection.

Another inviolate rule is that no resident subscriber may have a WATS line in his home unless it is used for business purposes. Exactly why this is so has never been satisfactorily explained. The stock answer is that WATS is a business service exclusively for business customers.

Business co-ops may lease WATS, but farm co-ops can't. Beta Sigma Phi has several WATS lines scattered across the country, but the National College Fraternities Association has been repeatedly denied WATS service. The official position is that a potential subscribing group must have "visible" connections, whatever that means.

An infrequent occurrence, but one to be aware of, is that the company is obligated to provide—and the customer is obligated to pay for—adequate service. This means that the company is not about to let an overly talkative customer clog up the network by using an insufficient number of WATS lines. If the customer has an active inward WATS line and the company determines that the "busys"—those calls not getting through on the WATS line—are above the accepted norm, it has the right to either install another line or to disconnect the one in service. You have the right to choose between these two evils, but nothing more. Under this arrangement, the company is making you pay insurance against the failure of its equipment.

All in all, the WATS concept is one of the better ones the Phone Company has come up with. Properly used, it can save time and money and eliminate some superfluous business operations. But careful tabs must be kept on WATS for it to work to advantage. If WATS might have a place in your organization, run a toll study before ordering it. To run a toll study, divide the amount of money spent on long distance phone calls by the total amount of time. The dividend is the per-minute cost. Multiply by 600 to compare current costs to that of WATS. The company runs toll studies at no charge, but they have been known to fudge on the results to get the sale.

If the analysis proves positive, order the line so that it will be installed as close to the end of the month as possible. Because WATS billing generally runs from the first to the thirtieth, it is possible to cut the first bill in half by getting the line installed on or near the last day of the calendar month. Be sure to allow plenty of time because the normal installation interval is two weeks in larger cities; allow a day or two more in case the company muffs it. A good rule of thumb is to request that WATS be installed prior to the day you actually want the line in and working.

Other types of long distance services include private lines, foreign exchange lines, and tie lines. All of these are point-to-point services that have rare applications for anyone but large business customers. If there is a high volume of long distance calls between one office and only a few other places, the possibilities of a private line should be examined.

A private line is billed mile-by-mile, with a minimal monthly fee for the telephones at each point along the route. If a customer is spending $250 a month on long distance calls from his Chicago office to his office in Des Moines, he should consider a private line because the rate is less than what he now pays for long distance. Once the flat monthly charge on private lines is paid, the customer can talk as long and as often as he needs to without spending any more. Private lines are not restricted to one-point service, either. Dozens of locations can be linked on the same private line and contacted by selective signaling—available at additional cost—without interference from the other points on the network. Ultra-high-speed data can be sent by private line with proper line conditioning. It's a service that gets few complaints from those who use it, but because of the high usage condition that must be present to make it economical, it's not for everyone.

A similar type of service is foreign exchange, which allows a user to receive calls from a distant point with no charge to the calling party. In fact, the telephone number at the "other end" has a local three-digit prefix. (For example: Airlines use this service heavily. A Philadelphia telephone number used to receive ticket reservations is answered in St. Louis.) Foreign exchange service has what is known as a "closed end" and an "open end." Your end, the closed end, is the terminating point; the open end is the one in the other city. Anyone who has access to the open end can dial it like a local call, reaching your city with no toll charges. By the same token, the people at your end can call the open end with no long distance charge. "F. X." service is an excellent way to maintain contact in another city without the expense of maintaining an office there: The mileage rate is identical to that for private line service, and a customer can make all the calls he wants for a fixed monthly rate.

Tie lines are available only to customers who have PBX service. In operation, they work exactly like private lines in that there is a direct link between points on the network. However, they also allow the linked points to talk PBX-to-PBX. For example: A station user on a PBX in New York can call his Los Angeles counterpart, via the intercom, just as if the fellow were in the adjoining office. There is data capability, but it is not as good as that offered on private line. Once again, the mileage charges are the same as those for private lines and foreign exchange lines.

To many persons, the mileage charges on these point-to-point services may seem high, but in proportion to what is being offered, the reverse is true. As of mid-1976, the charges are:

High-density mileage	.89 per mile
Low-density mileage	$2.63 per mile
"Short-haul" mileage	$3.15 per mile[1]

These charges apply to voice-grade circuits, and the category your organization belongs in will be determined by the Phone Company. If the plan is to use the line for simultaneous data transmissions, the line will cost at least ten percent more.

Special Reverse Charge Numbers are a holdover from the days before inward WATS, but, surprisingly, many companies still use them. S. R. C. N.s are toll-free four-digit numbers that calling parties in a selected area give the operator in

---

1. [Applies to all 1-25 mile circuits.]

order to reach you. The S. R. C. N. holder pays for the call—whether he wants to or not—at station-to-station collect call rates. There is a small monthly charge for these numbers—known by various names around the country, such as "Enterprise" and "Zenith"—on a location-by-location basis regardless of the volume they generate. The major limitation of S. R. C. N. listings is that several hundred numbers may be needed to cover an entire state. If coverage of a large area is wanted, it can be done via inward WATS, but for low-volume limited area coverage S. R. C. N.s work quite well.

College towns won't accept them because of the fraud possibilities, they cannot be used for identification when cashing checks, and they look like discarded movie passes, but telephone credit cards allow subscribers to make long distance calls when they are out of change by simply charging the call to another number. Credit cards are a convenience item that limits the amount of time spent talking to an operator. Instead of explaining and repeating endless series of numbers into the mouthpiece, the customer simply says, "Charge this call to credit card _____. My number here is _____." Be sure the card is up-to-date; the codes change yearly, and all kinds of accusations are made if an attempt is made to place a call with last year's credit card.

Credit cards are nice for residence subscribers on vacation, but for business customers a more useful item is a special billing number. Special billing numbers are used like regular credit cards, but at the end of the month the calls made on each special billing number are itemized on the holder's telephone long distance statement. Special billing numbers are sold in groups of fifty for about $2.50 a month, and all calls are billed at station-to-station rates unless otherwise made by the individual. If a company has salesmen out on the road, S. B. N.s make it easy to keep track of each individual's long distance expense since the Phone Company does the accounting.

Customer Service

The business services offered by the company are designed to handle almost every need of the business subscriber, or at least to lay the groundwork for help to follow. The four main areas of business services are: traffic studies, usage studies, phone power, and directory services.

Traffic studies deal with quantity and quality and help determine whether the telephone system needs more lines by counting the number of busy conditions that occur daily on the equipment. To arrive at an average figure, these studies are run for a week at a time. If the lines are busy more than fifty times a day, the company will probably recommend installing at least one more line. If the number of busys exceeds 200, the company will demand that the customer put in more lines and there is little he can do about it.

Peg counts determine how many calls are made and received. Either a register is put on the equipment, or a business service observer comes out and counts the calls. The study is run for at least a week and the results of the peg-count study are combined with the results of the busy study to arrive at an overall conclusion.

Traffic observation is a boring task for the person doing the study because he does nothing but sit and watch the operator go about her daily chores. He times each activity and counts how often it is repeated. The results are combined with the peg count and the busy study to determine whether more equipment is needed.

One never sees most traffic study results. They are sent to the Phone Company sales rep, who reviews the information and takes whatever action he feels is necessary. When he gets around to talking to the customer about the results, he may show him the result forms if he feels the need of supplying proof of what he's talking about, but the customer can't depend on it. There is seldom any need for him to see the result forms, the company feels, because the company learned long ago that the customer becomes confused if confronted with too many facts. If a problem exists, the company will be sure to contact the customer. If there is no problem, it chalks up the time and money invested in the study to operating expenses and forgets the whole thing.

Usage studies of equipment are made to find out if a system

is big enough for the customer's needs. Equipment usage studies are made to make sure the customer gets the best possible use out of the equipment he has. Other equipment studies determine what is useless and can be done away with during company economy drives.

Physical inventories ensure that the customer has every piece of telephone gear he is paying for. They are not run unless the customer asks for them and, even then, the company may hedge if it has reason to suspect an overbilling. A customer should insist on a physical inventory at least once every two years, even if nothing in his phone system is changed in that time. And he should not let the company send him an equipment list to enable him to do his own inventory. Let someone from the company who *knows* do the work. By staying with the person and having him identify and check off each item as he goes along, overbillings can be found and corrected.

Long distance studies are made to find out whether long distance services have an application in normal business operations. The previously described toll study—done by hand—is the mainstay of the Phone Company's arsenal in this field, but there is a computerized study that does the same thing. An L. D. Usage Analysis lists each call on monthly long distance statements and itemizes them by destination. This study is used not only to explore possible WATS applications, but to justify private lines and similar services as well. One drawback of the L. D. Usage Analysis is that the study must be requested and set up in advance. If the customer requests a quarterly study, it may be six months before he gets the results.

Closely akin to the L. D. U. A. is the Usage Analysis of toll studies. By means of computer programs, toll study results are analyzed and several optional solutions are presented. The Usage Analysis takes into consideration such things as the number of days in the business month, the number of working hours per day, the busiest hours of each day, and the delay in call completion that the customer will tolerate. This information, along with the dollars and hours expended, is distilled to arrive at one optimum solution and twenty or so lesser ones. Studies of this nature are made for WATS, private line, and F. X.

Although most WATS customers don't realize it, a study of prior WATS use can be a great value in helping them decide whether WATS is worth the money. The WATS Usage study must be arranged for in advance, and there is no guarantee that it will be completed in the month desired. However, when the customer does receive the results, he will know exactly how much WATS is costing him as opposed to long distance. There is a charge of a cent and a half for each call listed on the study, but if the phone company sales rep can be trusted he can get the study free and show his client the results.

Although not a usage study in the strictest sense, Usage Prospecting is the framework upon which all services are built. Usage Prospecting is nothing more than a series of questions all centered around communications. "What do you buy?" "What area do you cover in search of sales?" "How many customers do you have and where are they?" "What are your long-range business plans?" At times it may seem that the questions are meaningless intrusions into privacy. The sales rep will tell you that he needs all of this information to make a recommendation "tailored" to the customer's needs, but actually a lot of the information is unnecessary and many of the questions are idiotic. There is an outside chance that the sales rep will later sell the information to interested buyers, or at least use it to his advantage in a later sales presentation to one of his customer's competitors. The customer should be very careful about what he says.

The inner beauty of Usage Prospecting is that the customer being questioned gradually becomes aware of problems he never knew he had. This is the overall purpose of usage prospecting: to make the subscriber aware of communication problems and make him want whatever the Phone Company is trying to sell. Even if there is no real problem, the company will do its best to make him think there is. Keep a critical eye on the proceedings. The customer should never allow himself to be talked into buying or leasing something he doesn't really need.

If, after Usage Prospecting and a plethora of L. D. studies, the company determines that no hardware is going to be sold, it may try to sell concepts. Beware of concepts; they can prove more costly than any WATS line ever sold. Conceptual sales come under the general heading of Phone Power.

Phone Power is an idea, and ideas are hard to sell—which, by rights, should eliminate it from the company repertoire. But the big advantage of selling ideas is that the company need invest no money to make a buck on the deal. If it can get a willing subscriber to put one of its ideas into practice, it is dollars ahead without the expense of installing equipment. The ideas work. Sometimes.

Everyone in business is aware that the phone, if properly used, can be a fantastic selling tool. What the company sometimes forgets to do in its eagerness to make a usage sale, as these things are known, is to tell the customer how to make the plan work after the company leaves the picture. The Bell System practice is to mark a usage sale "sold and completed" the minute the customer agrees that the phone can be a useful selling tool. If he leaps after the usage plan in a big way, investing time, money, and people in his effort to use the phone more effectively, he may end up out on a limb without anyone to help him back down. No one should ever jump on the Phone Power bandwagon until he's sure that all possible ramifications have been fully covered and accounted for. The company is big on usage sales because, as I have said, they generate profits with no investment. These profits—which very well could have been seasonally generated by the customer anyway, regardless of the Phone Company's sales expertise—can be listed as a separate item on the yearly sheet. By listing such usage sale revenue, the company then can reduce overall rate of return on various items that otherwise would be next to exorbitant. When the government orders the Phone Company to earn less than eleven percent annually, usage plans—along with land speculation and stock market investments—can help them do so.

Directory services vary from one area of the country to another. In some places, the directory services are not handled by the Phone Company but are concessionary services provided by outsiders. But the larger Phone Companies handle their own and generally do a less than adequate job. Ten percent of all directory listings in the classified section are wrong. Since the company limits its liability to the cost of the ad over a year's time, suing the company for all but driving a business into receivership is an exercise in futility. The directory sales staff works on commission and the pressure is on to generate sales—it's an area where the company actually and officially goes out of its way to oversell the customer.

Getting directories from other cities can, and often does, take as long as a year—if they can be had at all. Directory listings in other cities, even though ordered months in advance, often do not make it into the books. Directory service established prior to the regular directory printing can be a long nightmare of "I'm sorry, but the number you have reached is not . . ." and take weeks and months to correct. If there is one area where the Phone Company really needs to restructure the whole game plan, it's Directory Services.

The companies do offer services that come in handy, but the customer must be very careful to see that the job is done right. If he orders out-of-state directories, he must keep prodding the company until he gets them. If he has listings in other directories, he should make sure they appear the way he wants them to appear before the publication date. The order should be confirmed in writing if necessary. Never should anyone allow himself to be oversold on his local listings in the classified directory. Checking the listings of competitors, and remembering not to make a big splash in the Yellow Pages when there are other more effective means available, should be standard procedure, company advertisements to the contrary. Customers should purchase a listing that is easily seen and won't confuse readers with many phone numbers and cute pictures. If there is no chance of making the deadline for this year's issue, a new subscriber should be sure that the directory information service has all the information he wants them to have. If he changes his telephone number, he should make sure that such referrals are being handled properly. And if special directories are needed, shopping around may be necessary. Polk, Criss Cross, and other directory publishers offer services identical in quality to the Phone Company offerings at much lower costs. . . .

C. O. A. M. E.

Customer Owned and Maintained Equipment is looked upon by the Phone Company in much the same way men lost in deserts must view buzzards. United Business Communications, Litcom, Telcom, Stromberg-Carlson, G. T. E., Ericcson-Centrum, Norelco, and North Electric are swooping down on Bell System strongholds with enough money behind them to maintain a respectable Balkan War indefinitely. The company takes this threat to its security so seriously that it is actually doing something it has steadfastly refused to do for the past fifty or sixty years—give the subscribers what they want.

The equipment section of this book did not focus on specific items for one very good reason. The last two years have seen so many new systems come into the marketplace that a definitive description of Phone Company systems would be outmoded by the time you read it. For example: The Bell System, as recently as 1971, had only fifteen or sixteen serving equipment systems in widespread use, some of which had been around as long as forty years. By September of 1974, this list had mushroomed to more than forty. The new offerings are a direct result of the pressure created by what the Phone Company discreetly refers to as "the outside suppliers." The company lost lots of customers when the competition floodgates opened because all it had to offer in the face of transistorized electronic telephone systems were its old mahogany-covered step-by-step switchboards requiring an attendant.

Now all this has changed. "Customer sensitivity" has become the byword in dealing with subscribers. Training sessions on competitors' gear are being expanded, both in content and in the number of employees who attend them.

Special action groups are found in most of the company's larger offices to deal with customers wavering in loyalty. And, most important of all, the company is no longer shoving equipment down the customers' throats.

Not long ago company sales reps would tell a customer, "This is what we think you should have." Now these same reps are saying, "Just exactly what is it you want out of a phone system?" These remarkable changes happened because of the Federal Communications Commission's 1968 Carterphone decision.

The innocuous Carterphone is an acoustic-inductive device used to interconnect two-way radio systems with the telephone network. Striking down tariff restrictions set up over sixty years ago, the F. C. C. ruled that interconnection by means of a Carterphone device was legal. Since 1968, with the Carterphone decision as a precedent, some 200 suppliers of telephone equipment have sold over a billion dollars' worth of their gear in previously exclusive Phone Company territories. The Phone Company is still the exclusive supplier of lines, but nearly everything else can be and is out on the independent supplier's shelves for the customer to look at. Unable to exclude the competitor's equipment by law, the company found itself in unfamiliar waters. If someone had told the company ten years ago that it would one day have to bid on the free market to attract business, the president of A. T. & T. would have questioned the prophet's sanity. But that is exactly what is happening today. In all fairness, it must be said that the company is a fast learner in the ways of free enterprise. Public contact employees are constantly harangued about their appearance and their attitude—and severely reprimanded when either is slack. Falling back on its unbelievably huge money base, the company has rushed the development of new systems so fast that few individuals on the line know what is available. It has also developed computerized weapons to waylay competitors' proposals. If the company can lay its hands on a proposal submitted by a competitor, it is promptly analyzed on a ten- and twenty-year basis, and a dollar-for-dollar comparison of the competitor's and the company's system is made. Millions have been spent contacting customers who haven't talked with the company since the day they ordered their service. Booklets, folders, mailers, and bill inserts are leaving the company mailboxes by the bagful in an effort to head off the minions of evil with their sinister gear. But why is the company playing catch-up football? With the $60 billion and the experience of a century behind them, why is the company apparently losing the game?

The major reason is that for the first time since the bitter struggles of the last part of the 19th century, the company has been forced to consider something besides its damned network. With singular purpose, the company pursued the Perfect Telephone Network. Reliable high quality service for everyone was the goal, and, in spite of many setbacks and blunders, that goal has almost been reached. (Anyone who doubts this ought to use the telephone system of France.) There was little time for the development of frills while the Quest was in progress. And when the Carterphone decision hit, the company had staid but fairly dependable equipment. The competitors, on the other hand, knew that to beat something staid but dependable you had to have a gimmick. Consequently, they—not the company—were the first ones to market such things as: music while on hold, direct conferencing, direct inward dialing on small systems, transfer of calls on any type of call, and trunk-to-trunk transfer within PBX systems. They also made some purely technological advancements that even Western Electric and Bell Labs hadn't considered until the rush was on. When the company realized that this was not just a passing fad, it too started gearing up. But one doesn't turn a giant former monopoly around overnight. When the company finally did get going, the Competition was already far out in front.

(Another reason for the company's slow rebound was one that it had not even taken seriously—the irritation many customers direct at the former monopoly. Some customers have such an intense dislike for the company that they would literally buy tin cans and string if it meant that they did not have to deal with the only Phone Company in town any longer.)

The company fell short in face-to-face contacts with the Competition. The competitor's sales force was smooth and forceful; it had to be, since all its income depended on the sale. The company's sales team, on the other hand, had to overcome the inbred habit of telling the customer instead of selling him. The years of exclusive territory had left a plainly identifiable gap in this area. The company salesmen were also hindered by the fact that they did not have to worry about commissions on sales. The company long ago decided that to protect the customers from sales excesses, its salesmen would work on a straight salary basis. While the plan did achieve a large measure of success, it also made the sales force somewhat apathetic. With little incentive of their own, they found it hard to match the elan of the competitors.

The Competition also had an edge in the pricing of gear. The company's rates are fixed by state regulatory boards and are available for public inspection in any library. The Competition was free to set its prices privately and to change them with no warning. The result was that it would submit a bid, the company would submit a lower bid at its set rates, and then the Competition would immediately lower its price to a level below the company's. In a number of cases, this price slashing bordered on the absurd. Several customers not only got brand-new telephone systems at prices far below cost; their Telephone Company phone bill was paid by the Competitor as well. But by 1973, plain and simple economics had caught up with the giveaways. Several parent firms informed their telephone operations that a profit was expected—and the sooner the better. So ended the price war. As we look ahead to the late 70s, it is quite apparent that service will be stressed as much as cost. The company is being restrained by court order from giving away lines, and the Competition is forced by the profit motive to stop giving away telephones. The future is bright for the consumer. Even though he'll pay higher rates for equipment no matter whom he buys it from, the service after the sale should border on the fantastic.

The Competition may present itself to potential buyers in one of several guises. The salesman may be a direct representative of the outside supplier, he may be a representative of the manufacturer, or he may be an authorized representative of many suppliers and manufacturers. The men of this last category are known in the telephone trade not as manufacturer's reps, but as communications consultants.

Communications consultants make their living by improving telephone systems. In return for this service, the client pays them a fee contingent upon how much money they are able to take off the monthly phone bill. In theory this sounds fine. In actual practice, things gang aft a-gley.

Consider a bank that allowed a com-con to do as he wished with its system. He started out by changing its trunk lines from unlimited to limited service. He removed unnecessary telephones—it worked out to include every other one. He changed the answering position from a console-type operation to a smaller and more complicated cord-type board. He took out most of the six-button sets and substituted nonbutton phones. He saved the bank almost $30,000 a year—and completely destroyed its ability to communicate. Because the bank had signed a contract, it had to pay his fee, but it also sued him for damages. The bank estimates that it lost several hundred thousand dollars' worth of business—but its telephone cost was reduced.

Generally, com-cons work the small PBX market. These customers have large enough systems to have some billing errors hidden in the woodwork. Also, they have little contact with the Phone Company. Because the managements of these businesses have little time to worry about the phone system, a letter out of the blue stating that the sender (the com-con) can reduce telephone expenses generally draws a favorable response. One com-con refers to this as tuna fishing. He drops an unbaited hook in the water and the fish takes it without stopping to consider the consequences.

If a manager of a business receives such a letter from a com-con, he should remember there are always ways to reduce phone expense but that they generally result in poorer telephone service. If he can accept such a thing, fine. But the best way to handle the com-con is to let him come and inspect the system. Let him make recommendations, but stop him there! Then, with the com-con's proposal in hand, confront the Phone Company representative with the evidence. Let him defend the company's position—if it's defensible—and take it from there. The key to good telephone management is to go slow and easy. The man who jumps off the deep end usually drowns.

Assuming, however, that the client decides to go with the "outside suppliers," there are certain formalities to be observed with the recently divorced Phone Company. The following is a letter few Phone Companies like to see:

CERTIFIED MAIL #1234567
RETURN RECEIPT REQUESTED

Standard Telephone Co.
1234 N. Lake
Buffalo, NY 11112

Attention: Marketing Department

Gentlemen:

We have on this day entered into contractual agreement with the A. Jones Telephone System, Inc. for the installation of an interconnect telephone system.

By this letter we do hereby grant A. Jones Telephone Systems, Inc., and its authorized representatives, authority to act in our behalf in ordering any and all necessary services from the Telephone Company.

Please instruct your Marketing and Plant departments to cooperate in this matter by handling all necessary coordination through the A. Jones Telephone Systems, Inc. office listed below:

Buffalo Branch Office
2345 N. Lake
Buffalo, NY 11112

This authorization does not preclude our ability to act in our own behalf on matters concerning telephone service.

Sincerely,

ABC Movers
Stephen Schaub
President

After denouncing ABC Movers and tracing Mr. Schaub's questionable ancestry all the way back to the amoeba stage, the company will send a reply:

Mr. Stephen Schaub
ABC Movers
3456 N. Lake
Buffalo, NY 11112

Dear Mr. Schaub:

This letter will acknowledge receipt of your letter dated _____, advising that you have entered into a contract with A. Jones Telephone Systems, Inc., to install a non-Company telephone system.

We further understand that A. Jones Telephone Systems, Inc. is authorized to act in your behalf in ordering any and all necessary services from the Standard Telephone Company.

Please address further correspondence regarding your service to Lisa Webb, Room 1234, 12345 N. Lake, Buffalo, NY 11112.

Sincerely yours,

Nancy Lesh

cc: A. Jones Telephone Systems, Inc.

Further correspondence will be somewhat lacking in the Old World courtesy of the first two because the company and the customer are about to become warring factions. The A. Jones group, for instance, may neglect to tell the client what kind of interconnect device to order to make his new system compatible with the Phone Company network. If Mr. Schaub asks the Phone Company to install one without telling it what kind to install, the company will somewhat icily ask him to go back to his new supplier for the information.

The company still requires that all interconnect device requests arrive complete. With its own equipment orders, it may come back to the customer twenty times for the information it requires. But when it comes to outside suppliers, all information had better be there the first time around. As we will discover later, relations with the company after buying your own system go downhill awfully fast. . . .

Personnel Services

There are five groups of Phone Company personnel the business customer should be familiar with. They are: the service reps, the marketing reps, the B. S. I.s, the installation teams, and the operators. It is important to know how to come to terms with these people because each in his or her own way can make telephone management easier.

The service representative is the person to call when there is a question about the bill or when you need minor adjustments in your telephone system. She (ninety-five percent of them are she's) is also a convenient starting point whenever the customer is lost in the telephone maelstrom. It's important to know the name of the service rep for two reasons: First and foremost, should a need arise you know whom to call; second, if something goes wrong you immediately know whom to blame. The service rep has a difficult position to cover. She has to represent the company point of view, no matter how unpalatable it is, and she has to do so by phone. Besides this, she has little authority to make decisions or to give every situation the time it deserves. An average service rep has a daily caseload of thirty customer contacts, ranging from simple bill explanations (if there is such a thing) to threatening disconnection for nonpayment of accounts. She also takes innumerable orders for service besides performing the diverse clerical activities the company demands. She's being watched constantly—or, as it is known to the company, "service observed." Service observing consists of bugging calls to make sure she's not letting off steam in the customer's direction. There is a good chance of a third invisible party being on the line when a customer calls in, but no matter; the observing is there to *protect* the customer.

If a subscriber wants something from the Phone Company, his service rep is a good place to start looking for it. If there is a problem, she's the first one to call. Don't take out frustrations on her, however, because she probably didn't make the mistake—she's just the part of the iceberg that can be seen. If the customer's approach is reasoned, the problem has a very good chance of being rectified. Outraged or irritable customers often discover that records have been misplaced, no records exist, and so on. In any event, take careful notes of conversations (for God's sake, don't tape them) so that there will be a record of the conversation in the event that another problem arises. Get a firm price to prevent surprises on the next month's bill. Always get a firm commitment on the date and time the work is to be done.

If you are going to have one of those serious heart-to-heart talks with your service rep about some pressing matter, put a secretary on an extension to take notes and let the service rep know what's happening. It will help everyone to avoid a misunderstanding. If the service rep can't help because she's not authorized to do so, immediately ask to speak to her B. O. S.[1] If the B. O. S. can't rectify the problem, ask for the Unit Manager. Never let a dispute be put off until it's reached the second-level manager; ninety percent of all problems can be solved before you get that far.

Supposing that your telephone system is one of those complicated ones (and whose isn't?): what is needed is the conceptual-thinking marketing representative. The marketing rep is the Phone Company's equivalent of a com-con. He is supposed to devote enough time to the customer's problems to make his system work as it is supposed to. He'll run long distance studies, analyze phone needs, issue orders, and coordinate them with other departments so that everything goes smoothly. In rare instances, he'll provide special services not specifically covered by the tariff. It's a fortunate customer who has a marketing rep who will go to bat for him against his own employer, and there are such animals around and about. If the customer has good rapport with the rep,

---

1. Business Office Supervisor

refer all telephone needs through him. He may do nothing but refer the requests to the appropriate department, but that's what the object is anyway.

Customers needing help do better to lay it on the line without pulling the big magnate routine. The marketing rep routinely talks to the head men of a dozen or more companies, and nothing is more infuriating than the "I'm an influential S. O. B. so you better do as I say now" routine. Like all Phone Company employees, he can lose things, too. He's not on a commission, either. Whether he wins, loses, or draws makes little difference to him. Don't try to bargain; he's not in a position to negotiate. Giving him enough time to do the job right; calling before Friday afternoon to get something on Monday morning will generate good will that is invaluable. With a company as big as the Phone Phactory, such relationships can be helpful for years to come.

If a marketing rep doesn't do his job, complain. If he makes promises and doesn't keep them, if he leaves things in a lurch, calling the marketing rep's manager should take care of the problem. If this doesn't work, ask for the General Marketing Manager. One hundred percent of the business customer's problems can be solved at this level.

Business Service Instructors (B. S. I.s) don't try to sell a thing—they just make recommendations. All things considered, these people can do more for a businessman than anyone else, as far as the phone system's operation is concerned. They are the ones who institute studies of the phone system's operation, train operators, teach employees how to make the system work, conduct classes on telephone use, and show employees how to make the system more effective. If necessary, they will spend days at business locations doing everything possible to bring the customer and the telephone system together. The difference between the marketing rep and the B. S. I. is that the marketing rep will tell a customer how to achieve more efficient communications and the B. S. I. will help him do it. In three years of research, never once did I hear a bad word about a B. S. I.

Business customers have more contact with the operators than with anyone else in the Phone Company. And of course, by the same token, operators have more contact with customers than anyone else in the Phone Company. The average operator handles one call a minute, seven hours a day, 242 days a year. There is no room for the personal touch when everything the operator does while on the job is regulated. From the words she speaks to the places she goes, no one in the company has it as tough as the operator. She works holidays and nights, her every move is "service observed," her absences are documented, her lunch hours and breaks are rigidly timed, she works with equipment older than she is, and the customer harassment is the worst received by anyone in the company. With these conditions to put up with, no wonder sixty percent of all operators quit in less than two years. If a customer has a problem with an operator, he'd better handle it while he's got her on the line because she's just one of several hundred on duty at any given moment. Her S. A.—service assistant—will handle unusual situations if she can. Beyond that, the person to talk to is the group chief. But, as I said, chances are pretty slim of getting anything done. If it's necessary to call back, it's like trying to find a needle in a haystack. The only chance an irate customer has is to try to psych out his problem immediately, before she thinks to disconnect him. Fortunately, operator problems are rare. More operators have been a help than will ever be a hindrance.

Installation people are not supposed to have much interaction with the customer, but a curious subscriber can learn a wealth of things if he listens to them. Unfortunately, most of these things are wrong. Installation—or plant—men receive little training in the way of person-to-person contact, and beyond what they have to know about the equipment, they receive little background information. But while they're installing equipment, they have a tendency to throw out offhand comments that can cause riots. One installer in the Midwest, while putting in a complex network of WATS equipment, told the customer that what he was installing wasn't what the customer needed. The installer had been around so much that he had come to be like an old, trusted friend. The customer believed him and immediately withdrew the order. The result was that a year's worth of Phone Company study and planning was thrown out the window. The sad part was that the customer lost the chance to save $24,000 a year in long distance expense.

The installers are nice, affable guys who install equipment. If they were salesmen, they wouldn't be carrying screwdrivers. Let them do their job. If changes need to be made, tell them what needs doing and they'll do it. Let them work unmolested and let them go about their merry way; they'll get the system in. But never let them try to sell you something else. They don't know what the order was except in the most general terms. They can be the Phone Company's version of the hidden flaw that Murphy talked about. If a subscriber thinks the installers are not doing the job, if they get insulting, if they mutter constantly with the subscriber as the target, the customer should get in touch with the installation foreman or the marketing rep and let him straighten them out. The installer is there to put in the system the way the customer wants it, not to criticize him for leasing a system the installer doesn't know how to install.

Section V: THE FUTURE

It is morning. You look out your bedroom window and see the powdery residue of the worst blizzard of the year. Not wishing to venture out on such a day, you decide to let your telephone do the walking. . . .

The Dream

Your first call of the day is to your landlord. When he answers, you tell him about the warped tile in the hallway. To emphasize your point, you show it to him via the phone TTV[1] monitor in the hallway. Because you're too busy explaining the situation to notice, the landlord must focus the picture from his end, but no matter. Since he can see what needs to be done to your tile, he already has made an accurate assessment of what is needed to correct the problem and how long it will take to do the job. In fact, since the introduction of TTV, you've seldom had to go into great detail when describing anything. If you find yourself at a loss for words, you simply switch on the TTV monitor and the party on the other end can see exactly what you are talking about.

Your next call is to the supermarket. Because you know exactly what you need today, there is no need to talk to anyone so you dial directly into the store's order computer.

1. Telephone Television. Bell refers to TTV as Picture Phone.

From a programmed list of items supplied to all regular customers, you place your order by pushing buttons on your telephone. When the order sequence is finished, you merely push
the phone buttons as they correspond to your bank account
number. The money will automatically transfer from your
account to the supermarket's. Your order will be delivered
this afternoon, and a complete list of the items bought and the
prices paid will appear on your regular month-end statement.

You have a few items to pick up at a local department store.
After dialing into their order system, you dial in the stock
numbers of the items you want. Once again, you give the computer your account code and the transaction is completed—
almost. There is not quite enough money in your cash account
to cover the cost of your purchases, and although the store's
computer will not complete the transaction until you resolve
the matter it is willing to wait. You put the store on hold, dial
your bank, and transfer money from your savings account to
your cash account. Then you return to the first call. The store
computer, having already noted the transaction, thanks you
and hangs up.

A neighbor calls and asks if you will take calls for her while
she is out. You agree, and your neighbor dials your number
again, after pressing one of the nonnumbered buttons on her
phone. Now all calls to your neighbor's telephone will ring in
your home until either you or your neighbor releases the call-
forwarding arrangement by pushing the other nonnumbered
button.

A friend from out of town is within visiting distance and
calls to ask for directions. You turn on the TTV monitor once
again and draw him a map that he can see and copy.

You've had a problem with some kids in the area who think
it's really grand to call you at four in the morning. You call the
Phone Company and have a pen register attached to your line.
Now all calls coming into your home will be recorded by the
time and date received and the number where the call originated. You receive two more calls from the kids before they
are caught.

These equipment features are not examples of what may be devised in the future, they are options that could be made available to you now. In most cities with populations over half a million, equipment capable of doing everything just described is in place now. The reasons you will not have such services tomorrow morning are by turns complex, ludicrous, and outrageous.

"We Have Met the Enemy, and He Is Us"

In 1970, amidst much fanfare, the Bell System launched Picture Phone service in New York, Washington, Chicago, and Pittsburgh. From Bell's 195 Broadway bunker came a modest prediction:

> By 1975, there will be at least 100,000 Picture Phones in two dozen cities from coast to coast![1]

Bell executives could hardly wait to count all the revenue sure to come from their greatest innovation since the inception of do-it-yourself dialing. They are still waiting.

Somehow, Bell's little moneymaker failed to make the grade. Of the original thirty-five Picture Phones installed in the Pittsburgh area, only five were still in service four years later and their days were numbered. All sixty in the Washington area were gone by mid-1973, and a similar attrition ratio held true in the other two cities.

"The Picture Phone is an idea ahead of its time," said a Bell spokesman. "It hasn't died, it's just sort of dormant." That the Picture Phone was an idea ahead of its time, and that it will someday be revived, is certain. Exactly when that day might be is something no one is willing to talk about officially. But, as one Bell executive jokingly observed, the general feeling is that it will reappear shortly after Christ returns.

The problem, as he saw it, was that Picture Phone was overpriced and superfluous. "In Pittsburgh, the installation cost was $150. The monthly rate was $160 for the first thirty

---

1. Bell Telephone press release, July 1, 1970.

minutes of use and 25 cents a minute thereafter," he told me. "Very few customers could afford it, for one thing. For another, Picture Phone can't do anything a telecopier can't do more accurately except catch people sleeping at their desks. A picture may be worth a thousand words, but it sure isn't worth two grand a year."

He gave another reason that stands head and shoulders above the other two: "They started out with this big grandiose plan to put thousands of Picture Phones in cities all over the U. S., when all of a sudden they discovered that the equipment will never handle it. It never dawned on them that a machine invented in 1969 isn't going to work too well with backup gear installed in 1939."

This is a major stumbling block in the path of many telephone innovations, and all Telephone Companies have to contend with it. But the cold, hard fact is that you can't tear out millions of pieces of gear simply because it's getting along in years. Updating telephone switching systems involves time, money, and something to put in the place of what you had. Many Telephone Companies have none of these three factors, and so will continue to use what they have until it dies of old age. How long that will take depends. After all, the Strowger Switch is still in use—and it's pushing ninety.

The progress of telephone technology is caught in a true Catch-22: Innovations require new types of backup equipment, from switching gear to wiring plans, and such things require time and money. Assuming that the money and time are found and invested, that's it for a while; the company then can't afford to make any other changes for years to come. If another technological breakthrough is made in the meantime, it will either have to adapt—which Picture Phone couldn't— or wait until another revamping is scheduled. Telephone Companies are true Sons of Thrift in that they will either make do or do without. Potential offerings are offered only up to the limits of capabilities. If these capabilities run a poor second to customer demand, then the company must either discourage interest by overpricing the item or live with the resulting they-don't-give-a-damn clamor. From the company's point of view, it's far better to live with a white elephant than it is to live with bad publicity. How much better for Bell to say that Picture Phone was ahead of its time than to admit that its central office equipment is out of the Dark Ages.

Because of long-term investments and chokingly high overhead, we will have to live without the wonders of a completely telephone-oriented society for the time being. It is doubtful that we'd want them if we had them.

The Telephone Society described earlier would put great pressure on us to be honest and upright—no more writing checks on Wednesday and making them good on Friday. With our propensity for cutting corners and attempting to "get away with it," we'd soon find ourselves in a fiscal morass of our own creation. Even more important would be our loss of individuality. In an existence tied to computers by account codes and pass numbers, those isolated computer errors we now joke about would take on new significance. A mistake in such a society might cause us to starve or get us arrested.

In any event, the progress of telephone technology is definitely going to be a gradual occurrence. Although some urban areas can certainly expect to reap a rich harvest of new services within the next decade, other parts of the country can expect no new services until the old equipment breathes its last. Based on past performance, this could take three quarters of a century. . . .

War and Peace in Fifty Seconds Flat

The IBM Corporation has computers on the market today capable of handling information at the rate of 500,000 bps.[1] To be sure, there are not many of these in use, but there are some—and more are sure to follow. Much more common are the 50,000 bps models. These are far from obsolete, but by the sixth generation of computer science (we are now midway between the third and fourth), machines with million-bps ca-

---

1. Bits Per Second. In standard usage, eight bits equal one character and five characters equal one word. Therefore, 500,000 bits per second means that information is being recognized at the rate of 12,500 words per second. At such a speed, Tolstoy's *War and Peace* could be handled in its entirety in fifty seconds' time.

pabilities are predicted by the most conservative systems engineers. There's a massive fly in the ointment, however, one that may slow computer progress to a slow crawl. It's the good old reliable Phone Company.

The idea of bits per second needs a little clarification here, because 50,000, 500,000, and 1,000,000 bps are not terms to be tossed out flippantly. Some people might assume that such speeds are achieved when computers "talk" to people, which is not the case. Such speeds are only possible when computers communicate with other parts of the same system. The problem we're concerned with arises when those parts are kept in different places.

Computer technology has had notable success in designing ever faster systems, and progress has been evenly divided between input and output units. There would be no advantage in having a faster output unit if you didn't have an input system able to receive information at an equal rate. The only straggler in this march of progress is the means by which the information is sent.

It does no good to invest in ultra-high-speed computer hardware if you can only transmit information at a rate roughly equal to the speed attained by a well-oiled teletypewriter. Let's say system A is spitting out information at 50,000 bps (1,250 words per second). System B is capable of receiving the information at a like speed, but in between these systems is a telephone transmission line that top ends at 7,200 bps (180 words per second). What happens is that the information backlogs. If every part of this small system were at parity with every other part, the entire transmission sequence could be handled in less than one minute (assuming that the content of this book was what was being sent, for instance). But because of the small problem in the middle, the send time is actually closer to eight minutes. Perhaps money is being saved by the use of computers. But a lot of money is being spent getting the message from one place to another.

In fairness to the Phone Company, it is only right to add that you can lease lines capable of handling the higher bps rates. Prices start at $645 a month for terminal equipment able to take 50,000 bps and go as high as $935 a month if you want to increase the capability to 230,400 bps. Keep in mind that these are the prices for equipment needed at each end of the circuit. In other words, you'll need two, so double the price. The line itself must be "conditioned" to handle such high speeds since regular telephone circuits cannot handle anything faster than 2,100 bps (52 words per second). This is now being outrun by its own brainchild. . . .

Hash

With the advent of competition, the Phone Company found itself being forced to expand its basic line of equipment. From a few items noted for their interchangeability, the list has mushroomed to the point where there is a veritable glut of equipment available. No longer will one item be a workhorse for many systems. Because of the bountiful supply, each system will have specific requirements that can be met—just as the publicity would have us believe—by exclusively designed gear. If the company ads are to be trusted, then we should never again find ourselves in the position where we must overlease in order to get what we need.[1] Or will we?

A recent Bell System ad of the "We hear you" genre shows us sixteen pictures of what it would like us to believe are sixteen different pieces of recently developed equipment. Of the sixteen pictures in the ad, eleven show telephone gear that has been available for ten years at least. Four of these illustrations show two of the same items, the differences consisting of dials on two of the items and push buttons on the other two. Still other pictures feature identical pieces of equipment with miscellaneous "extras" attached, presumably to give the impression that all are distinctly individual items. As if this weren't enough, at least two of the pictures show equipment that has been repackaged in the preceding two years—equipment that should have been repackaged in the early six-

---

1. In many areas if you want odd multiples of equipment, you must pay for more than what you need, since telephone equipment comes in multiples of six. If you want seven, you must lease for twelve, and so on. There is no price discount, either. You pay the full amount even though you may need only one sixth of it.

ties when it was approaching its fifteenth year of service. Simply stated, of the sixteen photographs, only three contain items that can be considered genuinely "new" or, as the ad proclaims, "the latest." The rest of the pictures show the same old hash, rehashed.

This ad illustrates on a very limited scale what the Telephone Company is up to on a very large scale—repackaging, adding to, changing around, and, in rare instances, inventing. I mentioned earlier that the company had added approximately thirty new types of systems to its line, and this is true. But many of these are new only in that they have never before been offered in the configurations now available. What has happened is that the company has taken material already on hand and joined it in such a way that it can truthfully be called a "new offering." To throw a cloak of respectability over these proceedings, the company, pathetically addicted to the habit of assigning numbers to everything that moves, gives these hybrids new identification numbers intended to mask the scent of crossbreeding.

One wonders why it took an Act of Competition to force the company to do these things. If these products were available prior to the Carterphone Decision—as most of them were— then the matter becomes a powerful indictment of the company's "public be damned" attitude.

And even the company's new equipment is nothing more than a reflection of what its competitors are up to. For example: a full three years before the Bell System offered its ten-button telephones[1], at least four of its major competitors offered one in many ways superior to the one Bell now has. Music on hold, a standard feature on many interconnect systems as early as 1969, was not offered by Bell until late 1973 in its larger territories. Music on hold has yet to appear systemwide.

"Time was when Bell was the leader," one Bell executive told me. "Nowadays, all we seem to be doing is playing catch-up ball to the interconnects [phone competitors]. We're not in front of anyone who is in the position to compete with us na-

---

1. Bell has offered ten- and twenty-button sets in selected areas.

tionwide." This sentiment was expressed often. A Litton Systems manager took the other position: "Sure, we're in front of them. And the reason is simple. While Bell and General were dictating terms, we were out in the field finding out what it was the customers wanted."

This seems to be the crux of the problem. Bell and its companies found themselves being ungraciously preempted by a horde of upstarts with gimmicks that worked. In order to maintain their preeminent position, it became necessary to actually do something about customer desires. But because it takes time to catch up, the companies have been forced to rely heavily on advertising that emphasizes developments while they are serving the same old meal. The only thing new has been the pot it's cooked in.

Now we are coming to the end of this interim era. The new systems—such as they are—are beginning to crop up all across the country. If nothing else, Bell advertising is much closer to the truth than it was in the beginning. The customer can hold out some hope of eventually having genuine improvements come his way. He can continue to have hope as long as the competition maintains its lonely struggle for the business the company has abused for so long. The new company systems, in some cases, will be part of package deals with temptingly low rates to attract customers and circumvent tariff structures. These innovations will be housed in cases that look like the control modules out of *2001: A Space Odyssey.* They will have fancy little extras thrown in to spice the deal, such as canned music for those lost in the fourth dimension of Hold, and they will have all sorts of improvements internally so that when someone calls out he might actually reach his party, and vice versa. The space requirements for these new offerings will be much smaller as more compact electrical components replace the gargantuan pieces now being used. The lease arrangements may go the way of the buggy whip, in that a customer might be able to buy outright everything from the switching gear to the lights in the dial. Although the company has been forthrightly opposed to such things in the past, there are signs that the bastions are crumbling. Several large Phone Companies are now selling hotel-motel services, and several ordinary phone systems have been sold in the Middle West. The implications of such actions go far beyond "new services" and "customer sensitivity"....

Getting Away From It All

An idea that has been kicking around for some time is worth mentioning in passing, if only because it might solve most telephone problems we now have. It's a simple idea, an attractive idea, and one that the bigger companies have taken halting steps toward.

Essentially, the Phone Company should get out of the telephone market. If the Phone Company did take this giant step, it would lose about half of its annual income, but it would also lose two thirds of its overhead. Equipment revenue represents 54% of the company's income, but it also represents about 85% of its overhead through maintenance, manufacturing, and personnel costs. By getting away from equipment sales, the company's profit would be less but the margin would be higher.

Such a move would benefit the customer. He would be able to get everything he wanted without suffering from the effects of shabby sales practices (on the part of the company and its competitors) or his own ignorance. He would still have to give the Phone Company its due every month, but he would have the satisfaction of knowing that he wasn't entirely a captive of the company. He would have a choice.

The major Telephone Companies could set standards that all suppliers of phone equipment would *have* to meet before their equipment could be offered. In this way, we could dispense with the ludicrous concept of couplers and connectors that now make a farce of the tariff. Penalties for failure to meet these standards could be along the lines of disbarment or revocation of license. Such penalties could be enforced.

The equipment suppliers would most certainly pick up the slack in manufacturing—few people would lose their jobs. Plant people in the Telcos (i.e., installers, repairmen, station installers, etc.) would not be deprived since the demand for such crafts would actually increase. The companies always have fewer qualified plant people than they need, and the competitors are always trying to lure company personnel over to their side.

The services of the future might become available sooner. Since the Telcos would not have the overhead, they might be able to find the time and money to get backup equipment ready. The equipment suppliers would have capital to develop new services, and the impetus of competition would make such a move a virtual necessity. Bell Labs, or something akin to it, could be established to oversee the coordination of such developments.

In the forseeable future, it will never happen.

For one thing, the Telephone Companies are not geared to thinking along such lines. The equipment sales they've made so far have only been "experimental." While they'd like to see the profit margins that would most assuredly result from such a move, they'd like to see it happen without losing the equipment market. Asking the company to surrender the equipment market is akin to asking Catholics to give up the Pope. No way is it going to happen. While the loss of overhead is an attractive thought to the company, the subsequent loss of profit is feared like the pit of Hell.

The consumer is not going to support such a move because he fervently believes all that balderdash the company has thrown at him about reliability and service. Besides, if the consumer had to find his way in the wilderness of phone equipment, he'd die of overexposure. Another overriding concern of the consumer is that such a move would mean a capital investment on his part. It would also be complicated. Imagine having to pay one company for the line, another for the phone, another for the lights, and still another for the bell. . . .

The employees would never go for the idea in a big way because, by and large, they are a security-minded bunch. They're in love with full Blue Cross-Blue Shield, pensions, and semi-annual wage increases. A wild and wooly phone market would mean a loss of security. No longer would the dunderheads get automatic raises, and their unions would have to start acting like unions.

The Phone Companies wouldn't come up with new backup services, citing lower profits as the reason. Never mind that their margin is two times what it used to be, the actual dollar figure would be lower. And since they would still have as many stockholders as they had before, they would have to cut expenses even further to keep earnings up. The equipment suppliers wouldn't come up with new services because the Phone Company couldn't make them work even if it had them.

It was just an idea. . . .

Phone Company Unification

This possibility is unlikely because of too many special-interest groups, too much diversification, and too little interest in the good service that would come of it. Besides, such a move would almost have to bring the government into the picture. . . .

Nationalization

Between 1917 and 1919, the Federal Government did control the phone industry. Since then, the most charitable historians have blamed the subsequent mess on the First World War. Others blame it on the Democrats. But the fact is that it was a fiasco of the bureaucracy's own making, combined with intracompany sabotage. Today, in those countries where the phone service is nationally owned, the service runs from poor to nonexistent. Would you want the government that gave you the Russian wheat deals, Defense Department overruns, Amtrak, and the Postal Service handling your phone problems?

APPENDICES

Appendix I: Sickies, Salesmen, and Other Weird Calls

The greatest disadvantage of the telephone is the anonymity it provides for the legion of perverts, salesmen, and other highly suspect callers who plague subscribers. By identifying some of the more common ploys, and the measures that can be taken to counteract them, perhaps some microbit can be done to halt the ever-growing problem of telephone abuse.

Obscene or annoyance calls are impersonally defined by the Phone Company as calls made with the intent to harass or annoy, or calls that are lewd and/or lascivious in content. In real life, the impact of an obscene call on the victim can be nothing short of staggering. The prank call, the vicious torrent of abusive language, the silent treatment, or the heavy breather can make for an unnerving experience at best. However, there are countermeasures that can be taken to alleviate the pain and damage to the psyche. All you need is a little knowledge.

Point Number One: The caller wants a reaction. He hopes that his call will create fear or outrage, and he usually accomplishes his goal. From his standpoint, the fear and shock value of his call make the risk of dialing worthwhile. The company has developed several methods of tracing his calls that limit both the vulnerability of the victim and the length of the caller's spree.

Many central offices are now equipped with tracing equipment that, in effect, freezes the call on the line even if the caller should hang up. Should the caller disconnect with such tracing gear in use, he will find the police at his door not very much later. New equipment in the central office cannot be counted on, though. New computerized tracing equipment is still the exception rather than the rule, so most obscene call victims will have to pin their hopes on standard tracing methods that are far less effective in real life than they are in the movies.

If the caller stays on the line long enough—say about thirty minutes—then he stands an excellent chance of being caught. If he should be so inconsiderate as to hang up within half an hour, then he's probably going to get away with it every time. Also, standard tracing works (when it works at all) only when the company has had prior notice. Since most obscene callers don't notify their victims of their intentions, the opportunities to establish a tracing network are slim.

Voiceprints provide a unique form of identification since no two voices are alike. Even if the caller disguises his voice, the voiceprint will tell every time. If it's available, a voiceprint can be the basis of an airtight court case. Unfortunately, like the standard trace operation, a voiceprint must be arranged ahead of time. Since advance warning plays such a large part in the Telephone Company's defense system, the victim of an obscene call is going to have to do what he or she can on his or her own during that first call. The most important thing to remember is that the caller wants a reaction, and the best thing you can do is to not give him one. In other words, remain calm.

The instant you identify the call as being obscene, the logical thing to do is hang up immediately. For what it's worth, the call should be reported to the Phone Company. The company might be able to catch the caller if he stages a repeat performance. Under no circumstances should the caller be kept on the line unless the company instructs you to do so to facilitate his capture. Keeping an obscene caller on the line on your own initiative might encourage him to pay a visit.

If the caller persists and the company is not helping out that much, then it is time to fight back. If a whistle is handy, blow for all you're worth right into the mouthpiece. If a whistle isn't handy, slam the receiver against the wall or floor. Some success has been reported with this method and the company does not make you pay for the smashed phone.

If the caller persists through all of this, on his next attempt simply depress the switchhook quickly and then say, "Operator, this is the call I want traced." Since the caller has no way of knowing whether or not he has been reported, he'll likely quit calling you and move on. He's well aware of the fact that he can go to prison for his antics, so he's not going to remain where his time is about up. Of course, someone else is about to get what you've just gotten rid of, but that's not your worry.

If it's any comfort, obscene callers generally do get caught, usually because they dwell on one target for too long. If the besieged victim cannot find any peace in spite of company and personal efforts, then it's time to change the phone number. A dollar a month for a silent number is a small price to pay for peace of mind, even if you should have a right to it free.

Since women are the usual targets of obscene calls, preventive measures ought to be taken. Directory listings such as "Jones, Jane M." or "Jones, J. M." are open invitations to the obscene caller. If you must have a listing, then use a masculine name. An obscene caller looking for a female will think twice before he calls "Jones, Jim M." If the Phone Company tries to discourage you from doing this, tell them why you want it and don't let them dissuade you with the last name and initials routine. The obscene callers are on to this, even if the company hasn't caught on.

No matter how you're listed—and even if you're not—you are bound to receive calls from telephone salespeople. Everyone has gotten calls attempting to sell products and some of these are perfectly legitimate—some of them must be—but the majority of the over-the-phone come-ons are pure and simple flimflams. Offering gifts, wonderful prizes, and once-in-a-lifetime bargains, the telephone con artists suck millions of dollars from the pockets of a gullible public at prices generally above and beyond the true value of the item offered.

Beware of "Telephone Sweepstakes" that want to give you "prizes" for answering simple "quiz questions." Be wary of accepting appointments with representatives of companies you've never heard of. Always check with the Better Business Bureau before agreeing to anything like this. Remain alert and ask questions, and you'll avoid a lot of grief.

If the voice on the phone does not clearly identify itself within ten seconds, hang up. If the first seconds of the call are garbled and rushed, ask the caller to repeat everything slowly. Find out where he or she is located. Ask for the company's phone number. Ask for references. If the caller is legitimate, he or she will be happy to do whatever you want. Aboveboard organizations realize that the hucksters have left a bad taste in everyone's mouth, so they'll go out of their way to be helpful and informative. Any firm that won't isn't worth your time and especially your money.

To better illustrate what you should be on your guard against, a few examples of telephone phonies from across the country are described below—a behind-the-scenes look at what happens in the $350-million-a-year telephone con circuit.

1. "Good evening. This is your Telephone Sweepstakes calling you from downtown _____. If you can answer our quiz question correctly in thirty seconds, you will receive (are you ready?) a beautiful 11 x 17-inch color portrait worth $20 for only $2.99! And if you answer within the first thirty seconds, you will also receive a portable Bar-B-Que grill absolutely free! Are you ready? Here's the question: What is the most widely read book in the world? (or) Who was the youngest president of the United States? (or—and this is for real) Who is buried in Grant's tomb?"

Obviously everyone with a third-grade education can answer the "quiz question" correctly—and generally within thirty seconds. Even if they don't, the anonymous voice of the "Telephone Sweepstakes" will tell them that they did. While doing the research for this section, I watched and listened while a young phone artist hit every house in his assigned territory using a street address directory for guidance. Using the "book" question, he received such answers as: the *Bible*, the *Encyclopedia Britannica*, the *Thoughts of Chairman Mao*, and even the *Amorous Adventures of Moll Flanders*. But no matter what the reply, the individual was informed that he was "absolutely correct" and subsequently "taken off the air" so that his name and address could be taken down. This information was relayed by phone to a delivery car stationed in the victim's neighborhood, and a coupon was delivered entitling the "winner" to a free Bar-B-Que grill or camera when he went to the photographer's studio that promoted the operation. But to get the "winner's certificate," the "winner" had to pay $2.99. When the winner showed up at the studio, he was presented with a cheap plastic camera or a Bar-B-Que grill half the size of a hibachi—and a hard-sell high-pressure sales pitch for portraits. While the victim could take his 11 x 17-inch portrait and his prize and leave, the average winner usually ended up buying $35 worth of pictures. In the meantime, the "Telephone Sweepstakes" moved across the state line at the urging of the local police.

2. "Hello, I'm from station W.H.I.T.E. We have selected your name at random to receive a free ham if you will allow our representative to deliver it within the next half hour. . . ."

Callers have used this come-on to sell vacuum cleaners with great success in the Midwest. They *do* give you a canned ham, and they *do* try to sell you a vacuum cleaner—but, according to the vacuum cleaner people, without the manufacturer's permission. The implication that they are calling you from a radio station and that they picked your name at random is a standard phony ploy in the business. Because most people tend to relate prizes and broadcasting, the "station W.H.I.T.E." grabs more business than would be found if the callers represented themselves as being vacuum cleaner salesmen. The "random selection" source is our old friend, the Crisscross directory. Every house on your block has received or is about to receive a call "at random."

3. "Good evening. Is this the _____ residence? Well, Mr. _____, our organization would like to know if you'd like to do something about water pollution and protect your family's health at the same time? . . ."

·This line, cast upon the waters by a water softener firm, stands as a classic example of what a flimflam ought to be. Everything in the sales pitch is 100% on the level. The catch? If you let them put one of their "pollution control water softeners" in your home absolutely free, you must use "Special Conditioning Detergents"—which only the sales organization can provide. The soap is available at a "minimum monthly charge" of only $17.50—for thirty-six months. If you agree to write a testimonial letter praising the water softener, the soap is available at a discount—$14.50 a month for thirty-six months. In the event that you try to sue when you discover that you've been conned, the letter you wrote will be entered as evidence for the defense.

4. "Hello. Is this _____? Congratulations, _____, I'm happy to inform you that you have just been named as a winner in our drawing. Do you remember signing up for it? I bet you thought you'd never win, didn't you? Our representative will be out to deliver your prize in person this evening. Will that be convenient? Good. We're so happy that you've won. . . ."

Wandering the streets of our larger cities are groups of neatly dressed young men who respectfully approach young women and invite them to sign up for a "free drawing." The prizes are "custom-tailored to fit in any girl's hope chest." More often than you'd suspect, the gullible females sign and, a day or two later, receive a call similar to the one quoted above. The "prize" is cookware. The girls do receive a small worthless item (i.e., potato peelers, salt and pepper shakers, tea holders, etc.) when the pleasant young man arrives. They also get a high-pressure sales pitch for a line of cookware that "will save hundreds of dollars over the next x number of years." As it is explained to the victims, the savings will be realized through reduced food costs. The cookware "reduces water loss." If the intended victim isn't interested in cookware, the company also offers glassware, silverware, and stereos—all "at prices below what you'd expect." Retail outlet pricing revealed the cost of the "drawing" goods to be at least twice as high as the norm. . . .

5. "Is this _____? Mr. _____, I'm with the _____ collection agency. Your account has been turned over to us because you haven't paid. Mr. _____, we're not going to fool around with you. Either you pay, or you've had it. . . ."

In spite of the fact that you might be the state's biggest deadbeat, the law specifically prohibits calls made with the intent to threaten or coerce. If you made a deal with the wrong sort of outfit, there's not much you can do if you signed a legal contract. But if the company calls you and uses threatening or abusive language, you've got a legal leg to stand and fight on. If you are called at odd hours of the night, if you are threatened or harassed, call the Phone Company and report it. However, if the collection agency is merely trying to collect a debt or notify you of their intent to start legal proceedings, then you can't do a thing. Any company has the right to try and collect what is due them, but they cannot be obnoxious while doing so. . . .

There are more—oh, so many more—ways that the phone hucksters try to take the public that a whole book could be written on the subject. So in closing out this appendix, here are a few points that would be well worth your time to remember:

1. If the caller launches into his pitch without identifying himself or the company he represents, hang up.

2. Be on the lookout for the "canned sales pitch." If the voice puts emphasis on the wrong words in the spiel, if the senten-

ces seem to run together, if the caller falters in midsentence as if he lost his place in the script, then he's probably reading everything word for word from a card in front of him. He's working the percentages. If he can sell his product to two people out of every hundred he calls, he can make a fortune.

3. Never sign up for free drawings. This is one of the most common methods of compiling sucker lists.

4. If you have doubts about the product or the company, call the Better Business Bureau.

5. If you feel that the item is worth buying, compare the price to that of similar items in the retail outlets near your home. Items sold by phone are notoriously overpriced—sometimes by as much as 350% of the suggested list price.

6. Be wary of any organization that wants you to sign a contract without first giving you time to think it over. The three-day "cooling off" rule might not apply, so be careful. Read!

7. Never buy an item to help the salesman "win a trip to Europe" or work his way back to Winnipeg. Sympathy ploys are old standbys in the rackets.

8. Remember that you owe this person neither your time nor your money. He called you. Have no hesitation about hanging up on him.

9. In 4,700 years of recorded history, nothing has ever been "absolutely free."

Appendix II: Telephone Regulatory Bodies

If you've got a problem with your telephone(s), nothing sparks action in your behalf so readily as a word from the Public Service Commission. Personal problems are best handled by a letter. Community problems are best served by petitions. For those with specific interests or concerns, public hearings are held at regular intervals. For the times and dates in your area, contact:

The Federal Communications Commission
1919 M Street N. W.
Washington, D. C. 20554

Alabama Public Service Commission
P. O. Box 991
Montgomery, Alabama 36102

Alaska Public Utilities Commission
1100 Mackay Bldg.
338 Denali St.
Anchorage, Alaska 99501

Arizona Corporation Commission
216 Capitol Annex
Phoenix, Arizona 85007

Arkansas Public Service Commission
Justice Bldg.
Little Rock, Arkansas 72201

Public Service Commission
State of California
State Bldg.
San Francisco, California 94102

Public Utilities Commission of the State of Colorado
1845 Sherman #500
Denver, Colorado 80203

Public Utilities Commission
State of Connecticut
State Office Bldg.
Hartford, Connecticut 06115

Delaware Public Service Commission
Dover, Delaware 19901

District of Columbia Public Service Commission
Cafritz Bldg.
1625 I St. N. W.
Washington, D. C. 20006

Florida Public Service Commission
700 S. Adams St.
Tallahassee, Florida 32304

Georgia Public Service Commission
244 Washington St. S. W.
Atlanta, Georgia 30334

Public Service Commission of the State of Hawaii
Box 541
Honolulu, Hawaii 96809

Idaho Public Utilities Commission
State House
Boise, Idaho 83707

Illinois Commerce Commission
527 E. Capitol Ave.
Springfield, Illinois 62706

Indiana Public Service Commission
901 State Office Bldg.
Indianapolis, Indiana 46204

Iowa State Commerce Commission
Valley Bank Bldg.
4th & Walnut St.
Des Moines, Iowa 50319

Kansas State Corporation Commission
State Office Bldg.
Topeka, Kansas 66612

Kentucky Public Service Commission
Old Capitol Annex
Frankfort, Kentucky 40601

State of Louisiana Public Service Commission
P. O. Box 44035
Baton Rouge, Louisiana 70804

Maine Public Utilities Commission
State House
Augusta, Maine 04330

Maryland Public Service Commission
301 W. Preston St.
State Office Bldg.
Baltimore, Maryland 21201

Massachusetts Department of Public Utilities
State Office Bldg.
100 Cambridge St.

Boston, Massachusetts 02202

Michigan Public Service Commission
7-Story State Office Bldg.
Lansing, Michigan 48933

Minnesota Public Service Commission
400 State Office Bldg.
St. Paul, Minnesota 55155

Mississippi Public Service Commission
1105 State Office Bldg.
Jackson, Mississippi 39201

Missouri Public Service Commission
Jefferson Bldg.
Jefferson City, Missouri 65101

Board of Railroad Commissioners of the State of Montana
(yes, Railroad Commissioners)
Capitol Bldg.
Helena, Montana 59601

Nebraska State Railway Commission (Okay, so it's a trend.)
1342 "M" St.
Lincoln, Nebraska 68508

Public Service Commission
26 Pleasant St.
Concord, New Hampshire 03301

Public Service Commission of Nevada
222 E. Washington St.
Carson City, Nevada 89701

New Jersey Department of Public Utilities
Board of Public Utility Commissioners
101 Commerce St.
Newark, New Jersey 07102

New Mexico State Corporation Commission
P. O. Drawer 1269

Capitol Bldg.
Santa Fe, New Mexico 87501

North Carolina Utilities Commission
One West Morgan St.
Raleigh, North Carolina 27602

North Dakota Public Service Commission
State Capitol
Bismarck, North Dakota 58501

Public Utilities Commission of Ohio
111 North High St.
Columbus, Ohio 43215

Oklahoma Corporation Commission
Jim Thorpe Bldg.
Oklahoma City, Oklahoma 73105

Public Utility Commissioner of Oregon
200 Public Service Bldg.
Salem, Oregon 97310

Pennsylvania Public Utility Commission
North Office Bldg.
Harrisburg, Pennsylvania 17120

Rhode Island Department of Business Regulation
Division of Public Utilities
169 Weybosset St.
Providence, Rhode Island 02903

South Carolina Public Service Commission
P. O. Drawer 11649
Columbia, South Carolina 29211

South Dakota Public Utilities Commission
Capitol Bldg.
Pierre, South Dakota 57501

Tennessee Public Service Commission
Cordell Hull Bldg.

Nashville, Tennessee 37210

Public Service Commission of Utah
330 E. 4th St. South
Salt Lake City, Utah 84111

Vermont Public Service Board
7 School St.
Montpelier, Vermont 05602

Virginia State Corporation Commission
P. O. Box 1197
Richmond, Virginia 23209

Washington Utilities and Transportation Commission
Highways-Licenses Bldg.
Olympia, Washington 98501

Public Service Commission of West Virginia
Room E-217 Capitol Bldg.
Charleston, West Virginia 25305

Public Service Commission of Wisconsin
433 Hill Farms State Office Bldg.
Madison, Wisconsin 53702

Public Service Commission of Wyoming
Supreme Court Bldg.
Cheyenne, Wyoming 82001

Texas Public Service Commissions are county-based and
therefore too numerous to list.

Appendix III: Glossary

The terms contained herein are words that make up a curious lingo known as "telephonese." The next time you discuss your telephone problems with a Phone Company person, you will at least know what he or she was talking about if not what he or she meant.

A & A Bureau: Abuse and Annoyance Bureau. The personnel in this line of work spend their time helping customers get rid of nuts, obscene callers, harassing collectors, etc. Should you receive "bothering" phone calls, get in touch with these people.

Blue Box: A device that enables the user to place long distance calls without being detected—sometimes. These devices are illegal, but used extensively nevertheless.

B. O. S.: Business Office Supervisor. She's the boss to all those disgustingly perky service reps. If you cannot get the message across to the service rep, take it up with the B. O. S.

B. S. I.: Business Services Instructor. A traffic employee who will come out and teach you how to use your phone system. An invaluable person to have stop by at least once a year.

B-Statement: The section of your telephone bill that lists all long distance calls billed to your number.

Central Office: A telephone building housing the equipment needed to keep an exchange operating. (In this sense, an exchange is any three-digit prefix area.) A central office may handle more than one exchange.

Centrex: A sophisticated telephone communications system enabling the customer to receive and make calls without going through a central answering point.

Communications Consultant: A person who sells telephone equipment and advises you about it, or who analyzes it. The term has gained new popularity within the Telephone Company but the independent operators use it more often (see **Marketing Rep**).

Commercial: A department within the company. Service reps and, in some companies, sales, are in Commercial. It is responsible for keeping up-to-date records on your phone equipment and billing, so that if a problem arises they can handle it or at least get the ball rolling.

Connector: A device to keep telephone recorded message machines from vaporizing central office equipment. Similar to a coupler, it is really nothing more than a glorified circuit breaker.

Coupler: A device used to prevent electrical flashback and maintain normal electrical flow on a telephone line. Used as a buffer between C. O. A. M. E. and Telephone Company equipment.

C. O. A. M. E.: Customer Owned and Maintained Equipment.

C. W. A.: The Communications Workers of America. One of the larger unions in the country, the C. W. A. represents 90 percent of the unionized Telco work force.

D. D. D.: Direct Distance Dialing. The lowest long distance rates available to the mass of humanity. Also known as One-Plus Dialing.

Decorator Phones: A generic term used to describe the pseudo-antique phones on the market—either Telco-made or otherwise.

E. S. S.: Electronic Switching Systems. Computerized central office equipment. Supposedly the panacea to all telephone ills and the backbone of those future services we won't enjoy for years to come.

Exchange: All numbers within a given three-digit prefix area. Can also be used to describe a geographical area the size of a city.

F. C. C.: The Federal Communications Commission.

Flat Rate: A single monthly charge for service.

Fuzz Box: A device that, by duplicating the tones of coins dropping down the phone chute, makes it possible to place calls from pay phones without using money.

F. X.: Foreign Exchange Service. A long distance service that allows you to make or receive calls in a given area for a flat monthly rate. Only for those who make or receive many calls in a relatively small area.

H. C. Instrument: An ordinary telephone with no extras.

I. B. E. W.: International Brotherhood of Electrical Workers. A union that represents seven percent of all unionized telephone workers.

Independent: A telephone company not associated with the Bell System.

I. C.: Installation Charge.

Installation Interval: The length of time between the date the service is ordered and the date the service is installed.

Interconnect: A supplier of telephone equipment. Telephone equipment not supplied by the local authorized Telephone Company.

Interstate: Telephone service that crosses state lines. Such services come under the jurisdiction of the F. C. C.

Intrastate: Telephone services that remain within the boundaries of a state. Such services come under the jurisdiction of the P. S. C.

Joint Practices: An inter-company guide akin to the Geneva Rules of War. The J. P. covers such things as intervals, offerings, and procedures.

K. K. 6: A six-button telephone. The standard telephone found in most offices, the K. K. 6 can handle five lines—the sixth button is used for hold.

Layout Card: Schematic drawings of the electrical circuits required for a telephone installation. Normally, you will hear of these only when they are lost.

Line: The electrical circuit terminating in your telephone.

Long Distance: Technically, any call that terminates more than seventeen miles from the source. Long distance is divided into three main categories: Direct-Dialed, Station-to-Station, and Person-to-Person.

Long Lines: A division of A. T. & T. responsible for the day-to-day operation of the long distance network. While the local Telco handles all maintenance, Long Lines directs overall supervision.

Marketing Rep: The salespeople of the Bell Companies. (Also known as Account Executive.)

Message Unit: Billing by the number of messages made on the line. Generally, the customers receive a flat rate for an initial period or amount and pay for any overage.

Mute Box: A device that enables the user to receive long distance calls without being detected. Use of such items is illegal.

Nonlisted Numbers: Telephone numbers that do not appear in the directory but that are available if the inquirer calls Directory Assistance.

Nonpublished Numbers: Telephone numbers not made available to the public. Also known as silent numbers.

O. C. C.: Other Charges and Credits. A statement that comes with your bill if you have had service installed or disconnected, "explaining" the fractional charges or credits thereof.

P. B. X.: Private Branch Exchange. Commonly known as a switchboard. Mini-central office equipment for business customers with from 10 to 2,000 telephones.

Phone Phreaks: People who use Blue Boxes, Mute Boxes, or other fraudulent means to make or receive long distance calls.

Phone Power: Concepts of phone usage designed to increase efficiency and/or reduce operating costs.

P. L.: Private Line. Unlimited calling between two or more points on one line for a flat monthly rate.

P. S. C.: Public Service Commission. A state regulatory agency.

Rate: The price.

Rate Step: Pricing based on increments. Example: Long distance rates are based on mileage. The greater the distance, the more it costs.

Revenue: Telephonese for income.

S. A.: Service Assistant. A nonmanagement employee who helps operators with difficult calls and maintains some semblance of order with the paperwork.

Service Representative: The young lady who takes your order for service, explains the accompanying O. C. C., and orders the service to be cut off when you don't pay for it.

Serving Vehicle: The equipment that makes your telephone system function.

Special Billing Numbers: A type of credit card that itemizes long distance calls billed to your number by the individual who made them.

Station: A telephone associated with a P. B. X.

Switching Gear: Central office equipment.

Tariff: The policies and laws governing telephone practices as set down by the F. C. C. and the P. S. C.

Termination Agreement: A contract required by the Telephone Company whenever a large telephone system is installed. A T. A. calls for you to leave a system in for a set length of time or pay a penalty for its premature removal.

Touch-Tone: The Bell System name for push-button dialing.

Traffic: A department within the company responsible for handling all long distance calls and maintaining order on all medium-to-large telephone systems.

U. S. I. T. A.: United States Independent Telephone Association.

Usage: The who, what, when, where, and why of telephone use. An in-depth study of your calling habits.

W. A. T. S.: Wide Area Telephone Service. A long distance service offered to business customers enabling them to use large amounts of long distance service for a volume discount rate.

Appendix IV: Long Distance Interstate Rates

On the following pages are the current rates for traveling by long distance. For ninety-four years, long distance bucked the trend of rising prices and went down instead. In 1970 they, too, started climbing. It will be interesting to compare these rates with those of ten years hence. Even so, there is no better means of communicating for so little money.

AM. TEL. & TEL. CO. L. L. DEPT.
Adm. Rates and Tariffs
32 Ave. of the Americas, New York, N.Y. 10013
Issued: March 7, 1975

TARIFF F.C.C. NO. 263
12th Revised Page 26
In lieu of 11th Revised
Page 26, rejected by
the Commission
Effective: May 6, 1975

LONG DISTANCE MESSAGE TELECOMMUNICATIONS SERVICE

3. SERVICE CLASSIFICATIONS AND RATES [TWO-POINT] (Cont'd)

3.1 Intra-United States Service—Schedule I (Cont'd)

(C) Rates and Charge Application (Cont'd)

(7) Rate Table (Cont'd)

(a) Dial Station-to-Station, Operator Station-to-Station and Person-to-Person

	Initial Period			Additional Minutes	
	Day	All Days, All Hours			Day
	Dial Station-to-Station	Operator Station-to-Station	Person-to-Person		All Classes of Service
Rate Mileage	Initial 1 minute	Initial 3 minutes	Initial 3 minutes		Each Additional minute
1-10	$.16 (I)(R)	$ .35 (I)	$1.00 (I)		$.06 (I)
11-16	.21	.45	1.10		.09
17-22	.25	.65	1.20		.11
23-30	.29	.80	1.30		.14

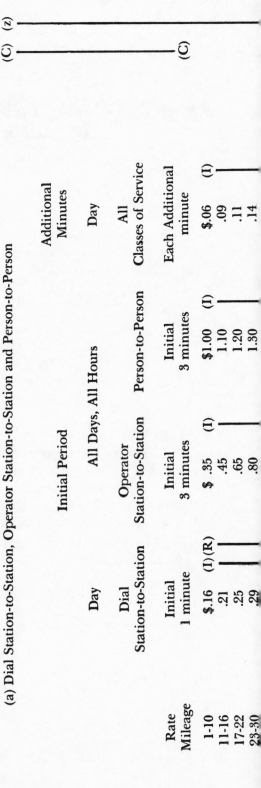
(C) ———————— (C)
(z) ————————

Rate steps				
36-70	.59	1.15	1.00	.21
71-85	.40	1.25	1.70	.25
86-100	.41	1.35	1.80	.26
101-124	.42	1.40	1.90	.27
125-148	.43	1.45	2.00	.28
149-196	.44	1.50	2.10	.29
197-244	.45	1.55	2.20	.30
245-292	.46	1.60	2.30	.31
293-354	.47	1.65	2.40	.32
355-430	.48	1.70	2.50	.33
431-675	.49	1.75	2.65	.34 (I)
676-925	.50 (I)	1.80	2.80	.35
926-1360	.52	1.85	2.95 (I)	.36 (R)
1361-1910	.54	1.90	3.10	.38 (R)
1911-3000	.56 (R)	1.95 (I)	3.55	.40 (R)

(N) ———————————————— (N)

(C) (I) (R) ———————————————— (I) (R)

(C) ———————————————— (C)

(b) Rate Discounts and Application Periods #

	MON	TUES	WED	THUR	FRI	SAT	SUN
8:00 AM to *5:00 PM	Day Rate Period FULL RATE						
5:00 PM to *11:00 PM	Evening Rate Period 35% Discount						Eve 35%
11:00 PM to *8:00 AM	Night & Weekend Rate Period 60% Discount						

DISCOUNTS

Discounts apply to total charges for Dial Station-to-Station messages and to total additional minute charges only for Operator Station-to-Station and Person-to-Person with total fractional amounts rounded in accordance with (C) (3) (d) preceding.

* to but not including

(x) Effective March 9, 1975 pursuant to Memorandum Opinion and Order (FCC 75-253) of the Federal Communications Commission adopted March 4, 1975.

Appendix V: Bibliography

Although a veritable mountain of research material exists on the subject of telephones, nearly all of it comes from periodical and pamphlet sources, thus reflecting the need for this book as well as the present dearth of hardcover reference material. The "book" material I did find proved most valuable and a listing is contained herein. As for periodical and pamphlet sources, I'm sorry to say that I only give credit to the publishers. If authors feel snubbed and insulted, I am truly sorry, but the sheer number of articles—and the brevity of most—makes individual listing impractical.

Books

BEYOND BABEL: New Directions in Communications, by Brenda Maddox. Beacon Press, 1972.

HISTORY OF THE BELL SYSTEM: An Introduction to the Bell System, by American Tel. & Tel., 1968.

I'M SORRY, THE MONOPOLY YOU'VE REACHED IS NOT IN SERVICE: by K. Aubrey Stone. Ballantine Books, 1973.

MONOPOLY. . . . : by Joseph Goulden. Putnam, 1968.
THE PUSHBUTTON TELEPHONE SONGBOOK. . . . : by
Michael Scheff. Price/Stern/Sloan, 1973.
TELEPHONY'S DIRECTORY, Annual Editions of 1970 thru
1974. Telephony Publishing.

Pamphlets

Bell System

"Annual Report to Stockholders," 1970-1974.
"Bell System Data Sets," 1973.
"Equal Opportunity in the Bell System," 1973.
"It's Your Move," 1972.
"Employees' Benefits," 1971.
"Your Place in the Bell System," 1970.
"Code of Conduct for Employees," 1970.
"Service Order Routing," 1972.
"Expense Coding," 1972.
"Sales Procedures, The Five-Step Plan," 1970.
"Initial Sales & Products Training Guide," 1970.
"PBX Sales Training Manuals," 1970.
"Organization & Policy," 1970.
"Customer Relations Policies & Procedures," 1971.
"Uniform Service Order Codes," 1970.
"Metropolitan Rate and Service Guide," 1968, 1971, 1973.
"Bell System Joint Practices," 1971.

Other Sources

"Annual Report to Stockholders—United Tel.," 1973-1974.
"Annual Report to Stockholders—Continental Tel.," 1972-
1973.
"What They Say About CWA," 1965.
"Communications Workers of America Agreements," 1971,
1974.

"History of USITA," 1971.

"Telephone Sales Techniques," 1964.

"Telephone Testing Procedures," 1968.

"The FCC," 1965.

"Your Telephone Company in Action," 1969.

Periodicals

"Telephone Engineer & Management," every issue since April 70.

"Telephony," every issue since July 70.

"The Phone Phreak's Last Stand," *Oui* Magazine, August 73.

"Regulating the Phone Company in Your Home," *Ramparts* Magazine, June 72.

"How the Phone Company Interrupted our Service," *Ramparts* Magazine, July 72.

"For Whom Does Bell Toll?" *Telephone Interconnect Journal*, February 74.

"Take That, You Soulless S. O. B.!" *Playboy*, October 72.

"Secrets of the Little Blue Box," *Esquire*, October 72.

"What It Costs to Communicate," *The Office*, April 70.

"Dormant Picturephone," *Parade*, August 18, 74.

"Goals that Look Like Quotas," *Time*, January 29, 73.

Telephone Times, every issue since January 72.

"Compensation Survey 71: Top Pay Soars," *Business Week*, May 6, 72.

"Top Fifty—How much they made," *Fortune*, March 72.

"Global Telephone Network," *Saturday Review*, October 28, 72.

"Phoney Tunes," *Time*, March 6, 72.

"Bias Charges in Hiring," *U. S. News & World Report*, August 14, 72.

"Ma Bell Takes Her Lumps," *Reader's Digest*, April 70.

"Rising Toll of the Telephone Hangup," *Time*, March 23, 70.

"Telephone Operator," *Atlantic*, October 71.

"Revolution in the Phone Business," *Business Week*, November 6, 71.

"Bell Labs Makes a Switchless Switch," *Business Week*, June 10, 72.

"Wages Rise Sharply for Telephone Workers," *Labor Review*, August 72.

"Autodialers Takes Ma Bell to Court," *Business Week*, December 2, 72.

"Own your own Phones," *American City*, August 72.

"Name Calling," *Time*, December 18, 72.

"Coming Shake-Up in Telecommunications," *Fortune*, April 70.

"Upheaval in Communications," *U. S. News & World Report*, July 13, 70.

"They're cracking down on phone nuts and you can help," *Today's Health*, May 70.

"Open Season on Telephones," *Business Week*, February 7, 70.

"Future Features," *Signal*, September 73.

"Teaching Telephone Techniques," *Today's Education*, February 71.

"Phone rates raise more static," *Business Week*, October 31, 70.

"The Bell System kids the Press," *Nation*, February 16, 70.

"Independent Telephone Companies with growth potential," *Fortune*, May 72.

"Out of Sight Info Center," *Mechanix Illustrated*, June 72.

"Loneliness of the Short Distance Dialer," *Esquire*, October 70.

"Why a Blue Chip has been fading; A. T. & T.'s long slide," *Business Week*, February 70.

"Working with the Unskilled," *U. S. News & World Report*, March 9, 71.

"The needless non-listed number," *Signal*, July 72.

"Look, Ma Bell, No Hands!" *Time*, May 4, 70.

"911 Covers All Emergencies," *American City*, November 71.

"What lasers can do for the phone system," *Business Week*, May 20, 72.

"The Telephone Scandal," *L'Express*, August 16, 65.

"It jus' growed," *Signal*, May 74.

"The effectiveness of regulation," *Law Review*, May 73.

"The invincible coin phone," *Signal*, January 72.

Newspapers

New York *Times*

Los Angeles *Times*

Houston *Post*

Cleveland *Plain Dealer*

Boston *Globe*

Kansas City *Star*

Wall Street *Journal*

Pittsburgh *Press*

San Antonio *Express & News*

Washington *Post*

Chicago *Tribune*

Dallas *Morning News*

Denver *Rocky Mountain News*

Detroit *News*

Fort Worth *Press*

Memphis *Press-Scimitar*

Philadelphia *Inquirer*

St. Louis *Post-Dispatch*

San Antonio *Light*

San Francisco *Examiner*

Washington *Daily News*

Miscellaneous

Congressional Record: June 73

F. C. C.: Transcripts of interstate rate hearings, February 72.

"The Federal Telephone System," U. S. Gov. Pub. 1972.

"Results of the Telethon," *Muscular Dystrophy Newsletter* August 73.

THE DEATH OF A PRESIDENT: by William Manchester. Harper & Row, 1967.

Telecommunications: An address by T. S. Kurnberger, pub. March 15, 72.

F. Y. I. & Interdepartmental memos of the Bell System.

ACKNOWLEDGMENTS

Without the help of many individuals, a book of this kind could not be written. All of my Telephone Company sources will be rewarded with anonymity for their candid observations. Their help was invaluable, and I hope they can help institute the changes both they and I would like to see. In passing, let me say that it's not who they are but what they said that's important.

I would like to add that if it seems that Bell sources are quoted more often than people from other phone companies, it's because Bell employees are more accessible and willing to talk. It does speak well of the company.

On a personal level, I would like to thank Kay Webb for typing and retyping the manuscript, Mouse and D. J. for their cheerful acceptance of my absence during the composition, Consiglieri Karen for her helpful advice and criticisms, and the Rug Rats for being there when I needed them.

INDEX